T0163081

Happy Quilter
VARIETY PUZZLES

Gailen Runge

60 + Large-Print Word Puzzles
for Quilt Lovers

VOLUME 2

C&T PUBLISHING

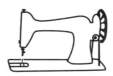

Contents

ctpub.com   P.O. Box 1456, Lafayette, CA 94549 | 800.284.1114

Copyright © 2018 by C&T Publishing, Inc. All rights reserved.

PRODUCT TEAM: Betsy LaHonta, Gailen Runge, Kerry Graham, Zinnia Heinzmann, and Jennifer Warren

We take great care to ensure that the information included in our products is accurate and presented in good faith, but no warranty is provided, nor are results guaranteed. Having no control over the choices of materials or procedures used, neither the author nor C&T Publishing, Inc., shall have any liability to any person or entity with respect to any loss or damage caused directly or indirectly by the information contained in this book.

COVER QUILT DETAIL: *Sisters Nine Patch* by Bonnie K. Hunter

Printed in the USA

10 9 8 7 6 5

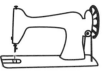

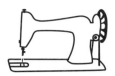

Instructions

Quilt Block Word Mines

See how many words you can make out of the letters in popular quilt blocks!

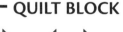

QUILT BLOCK

5-letter words (2)

b o i t e

t o w i e

4-letter words (2)

b i t e

o b i t

3-letter words (15)

b e t	o b i	t w o
b i o	o w e	w e b
b i t	t i e	w e t
b o t	t o e	w i t
b o w	t o w	w o e

2-letter words (7)

b e	o w	t o
b i	t i	w e
i t		

Word RoundUps™

Word RoundUps are a combination of traditional word search and crossword puzzles. Use the crossword-style clues to identify the hidden words.

Getting Started

```
S  B  X  Y  E  L  S  I  A  P
I  C  J  V  D  D  O  Y  T  T
U  V  I  W  E  A  G  A  H  X
P  Y  E  S  G  Q  P  U  L  B
O  N  U  S  S  M  L  U  I  P
L  D  Y  E  C  O  O  P  Y  C
K  W  R  I  E  K  R  O  E  F
A  T  Z  X  R  L  U  W  O  F
D  M  X  E  P  L  D  L  W  N
O  E  L  W  B  M  G  E  O  A
T  U  C  C  R  D  P  S  E  M
R  L  S  T  O  I  Z  W  G  N
```

 3 tools quilters use regularly

 2 fabric patterns that start with **P**

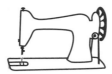

Word Scrambles

Who doesn't love a good word scramble?
Unscramble the letters to find popular quilting terms.

GIDNOI . . . . indigo

RWPOED BULE . . . . powder blue

VYNA . . . . navy

DHMTIIGN . . . . midnight

SHADES OF BLUE

◤ Criss Crosses

Like Word RoundUps, Criss Cross puzzles are a combination of word search and crossword puzzles.

The grid is like a crossword puzzle, but instead of clues, the words are listed as they are in a word search. Guided by the placement of letters where words cross, fill the words into their spot in the puzzle. **HINT:** *The easiest way to get started is to place words where there is only one option (for example, if there is only one word with three letters). If there aren't any of those, start with a letter grouping with few entries and compare crossing words.*

Quilter Activities

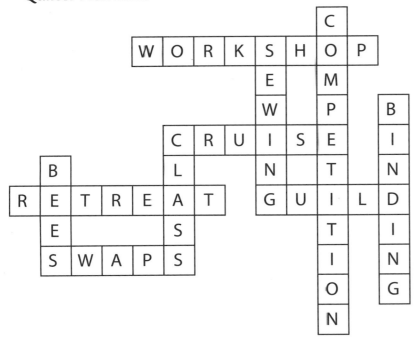

11 letters
C O M P E T I T I O N

8 letters
W O R K S H O P

7 letters
B I N D I N G
R E T R E A T

6 letters
S E W I N G
C R U I S E

5 letters
G U I L D
S W A P S
C L A S S

4 letters
B E E S

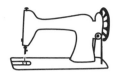

Logic Puzzles

Each logic puzzle is a simple story involving different elements, such as people, places, things, times, and amounts. Your goal in solving a logic puzzle is to figure out the relationship between the different elements. Each logic puzzle has a little background on the story and a list of clues. It's also accompanied by a grid that you can use to help solve the puzzle.

Read through the clues. Each time you learn that two elements are or are not related, record the fact in the grid. If the fact is something that is **NOT TRUE** (that Sue did not sew the pillow, for example), use an **X** in the grid. If the fact is **TRUE** (that the fourth speaker sewed the baby quilt), use an **O** in the grid. Use your deductive reasoning to eliminate options. In clue 1 below, for example, you know that Sue did not sew the anniversary quilt. You also know that the anniversary quilt could not be presented fourth and that Sue could not have spoken first because the anniversary quilt was presented before Sue spoke.

Work through the puzzle in blocks of related facts. When you eliminate all but one possibility for an element in a block, you know that remaining possibility is the correct answer.

Each positive answer will lead to more related facts, and you will deduce your way to solving the puzzle!

June Bug Quilt Meeting

For the answer to this logic puzzle, see Solutions (page 73).

At the June Bug Quilt Guild's winter meeting, four members showed their new work. Using only the clues that follow, match each member to the item she sewed and the order in which she spoke.

1. The quilter who sewed the anniversary quilt spoke right before Sue.

2. The guild member that spoke second was either Betsy or the quilter who made the wallhanging.

3. The maker of the wallhanging spoke two spots before Alice.

4. Kerry made the anniversary quilt.

5. The last speaker of the evening made the baby quilt.

		QUILTER				PROJECT			
		Betsy	Sue	Kerry	Alice	Wallhanging	Baby quilt	Anniversary quilt	Patchwork pillow
ORDER	1		X		X		X		
	2				X		X		
	3						X		
	4					X	O	X	X
PROJECT	Wallhanging	X		X					
	Baby quilt			X					
	Anniversary quilt	X	X	O	X				
	Patchwork pillow			X					

ORDER	QUILTER	PROJECT
1		
2		
3		
4		Baby quilt

- -

Crossword Puzzles

Solve the clues and enter your answers into the puzzle boxes, following the clue number and word orientation.

Word Searches

Search the puzzle for the words in the word list. Words can run forwards, backwards, up, down, and on any diagonal.

Puzzles

💟 Crossword Puzzle 1

QUILT PARTS

ACROSS

2 temporarily joining fabric together

4 folded triangles (2 wds)

7 the finishing touch

10 in a bind, again (3 wds)

12 quilter's quadrilateral

16 basic element of a policy or quilt

18 the solid fabric

20 hangs it up

21 holds it together

22 quilter's lunch?

DOWN

1 it's what's inside that counts

3 an added beauty

5 decorative element in a cake or quilt

6 building-block base

8 make your mark

9 lives on the edge

11 108"-wide yardage

13 building block of blocks

14 every patch pair has one

15 stacks in cakes and quilts

17 quilt top layout

19 single unit in piecing

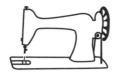

 Word Scramble 1

Unscramble the words to find popular quilting terms.

QUILT TYPES

UTRHGAOAP — — — — — — — — —

SRLEAPM — — — — — — —

LAMBU — — — — —

RCMHA — — — — —

IWIANHAA — — — — — — — —

LIEALOMND — — — — — — — —

T-SITHR — ´ — — — — —

NSITGR — — — — — —

PASRC — — — — —

EROMND — — — — — —

ORMYME — — — — — —

ACYRZ — — — — —

MARSCISTH — — — — — — — —

ILICV AWR — — — — —   — — —

GRA — — —

UROTAPNT — — — — — — — —

TRICLIOPA — — — — — — — — —

ATR — — —

MESNELIO — — — — — — — —

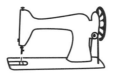

Word Scramble 2

Unscramble the words to find popular quilting terms.

FABULOUS FABRICS

DCBHALROTO _ _ _ _ _ _ _ _ _ _

IEMDN _ _ _ _ _

LEAFNLN _ _ _ _ _ _ _

KTABI _ _ _ _ _

ILHCEENL _ _ _ _ _ _ _ _

RYDROCOU _ _ _ _ _ _ _ _

MSNHPUOE _ _ _ _ _ _ _ _

ARJUCADQ _ _ _ _ _ _ _ _

AVGITNE _ _ _ _ _ _ _

ULSNMI _ _ _ _ _ _

TVEELV _ _ _ _ _ _

CETELN _ _ _ _ _ _

EDEF CSKA _ _ _ _ _ _ _ _

PTELORYES _ _ _ _ _ _ _ _ _

FCOHIFN _ _ _ _ _ _ _

FMROBREICI _ _ _ _ _ _ _ _ _ _

NINLE _ _ _ _ _

AADKSM _ _ _ _ _ _

OLWO LFTE _ _ _ _ _ _ _ _

HENRFC RETYR _ _ _ _ _ _ _ _ _ _ _

LSKI _ _ _ _

ULETL _ _ _ _ _ _

DRAGIENEB _ _ _ _ _ _ _ _ _

NMGGIAH _ _ _ _ _ _ _

TODDTE WSSIS _ _ _ _ _ _ _ _ _ _ _

ELETEY _ _ _ _ _ _

GNIKTCI _ _ _ _ _ _ _

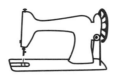

♥ Crossword Puzzle 2

ACTION WORDS

ACROSS

1   leave one's _____

4   the opposite of "to fly by the seat of your pants"

5   set the seam

7   knife-edge (e.g.)

9   tack on top

12   make perfect?

15   make laundry origami

16   incision or division?

17   one way to secure appliqué (2 wds)

18   stack

19   squaring up

20   hold it together

DOWN

1   judge the distance

2   frog it

3   to sew with toe-catcher–type stitches

6   make a template

7   Drunkard's Path (e.g., 2 wds)

8   to match up, as stars or edges

10   a combustible stick

11   the first stitch in any seam

13   secure trim

14   to slice with a circular blade (2 wds)

15   to glue in fabric terms

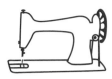

♥ Crossword Puzzle 3

IT'S A MATTER OF TECHNIQUE

ACROSS

4 look through semi-closed eyes

7 using paper for precision sewing (2 wds)

9 quilt a little now, quilt a little later ... (4 wds)

10 flatten an area that has been stitched

11 needs partial construction

14 sewing a partial seam (2 wds)

17 gluing with an iron

18 British hexagon sewing (abbr)

19 tack on top

20 use a seam ripper

DOWN

1 smooth, narrow thread technique (2 wds)

2 painting with a sewing machine and thread (2 wds)

3 to match up, as stars or edges

5 winging it

6 another way to hold it together

8 remove wrinkles from fabric

10 _____ makes perfect

12 making a template

13 make a diagonal square corner

15 make a block true (2 wds)

16 cut away excess

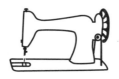

Criss Cross 1

HAND QUILTING

8 letters	7 letters	6 letters	5 letters	4 letters	3 letters
SCISSORS	BACKING	NEEDLE	CHAIR	HOOP	TOP
THREADER	BASTING	THREAD	TABLE	PINS	
	BATTING			TAPE	
	BEESWAX			TIME	
	FRIENDS				
	THIMBLE				

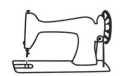

Criss Cross 2

COLORS

9 letters

CHOCOLATE

TURQUOISE

8 letters

BURGUNDY

7 letters

CRIMSON

6 letters

INDIGO

ORANGE

PURPLE

VIOLET

YELLOW

5 letters

AMBER   OLIVE

BLACK   PEACH

BROWN   WHITE

GREEN

KHAKI

LILAC

4 letters

BLUE

GOLD

GREY

LIME

NAVY

PINK

3 letters

RED

TAN

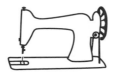

❊ Logic Puzzle 1

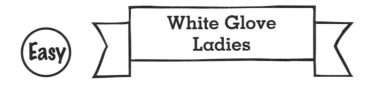

Easy

White Glove Ladies

Amy is training several new volunteers to work as docents, affectionately called "white glove ladies," at the Concord Annual Quilt Show. She needs to check on their results after their first full day at the show. Help Amy match each volunteer to her exhibit as well as the number of visitors she helped.

1. The 4 volunteers include the volunteer who helped 75 visitors, the volunteer who worked in the appliqué exhibit, the volunteer who worked in the wearable-art section, and Debbie.

2. Sue volunteered in the appliqué exhibit.

3. The volunteer who worked in the wallhanging exhibit helped 25 more visitors than the volunteer who covered the wearable-art exhibit.

4. Debbie helped fewer visitors than the person who volunteered in the appliqué exhibit.

5. Liz helped 25 fewer visitors than Debbie.

		VOLUNTEERS				EXHIBITS			
		Linda	Debbie	Liz	Sue	Appliqué	Modern	Wearable art	Wallhanging
VISITORS	25								
	50								
	75								
	100								
EXHIBITS	Appliqué								
	Modern								
	Wearable art								
	Wallhanging								

VISITORS	VOLUNTEERS	EXHIBITS
25		
50		
75		
100		

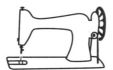

✳ Logic Puzzle 2

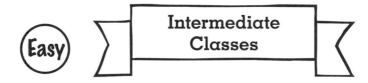

Intermediate Classes

(Easy)

Carolie taught a very successful series of beginning quilting classes. When her students completed the class, she gave each of them a pass to an intermediate class she thought the student would like. Using the clues listed below, match each of her students to the date of her next class and the subject of that class.

1. Roxane is either the student who took the class on July 18 or the student who attended the free-motion quilting class.

2. Roxane took needle-turn appliqué.

3. The fabric dyeing student attended class 3 days after Kristi.

4. Dawn took the sewing curves class.

		STUDENTS				QUILT CLASSES			
		Angela	Dawn	Kristi	Roxane	Sewing curves	Fabric dyeing	Free-motion quilting	Needle-turn appliqué
DATES	July 12								
	July 15								
	July 18								
	July 21								
QUILT CLASSES	Sewing curves								
	Fabric dyeing								
	Free-motion quilting								
	Needle-turn appliqué								

DATES	STUDENTS	QUILT CLASSES
JULY 12		
JULY 15		
JULY 18		
JULY 21		

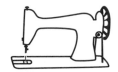

✦ Word RoundUp 1

QUILT QUESTIONS

```
Z  B  B  B  D  K  T  H  O  I  H  O  E  L  B  U  O  D
L  A  M  X  V  A  I  B  G  T  H  O  Q  X  I  Z  R  T
E  T  J  Z  D  P  T  N  F  X  J  F  U  X  E  G  W  F
M  T  R  L  J  C  C  P  G  E  N  G  E  J  Q  I  P  I
O  I  R  L  F  H  S  N  H  X  C  E  A  N  E  R  O
Y  N  I  A  W  X  K  Q  D  Y  N  G  N  I  K  C  A  B
N  G  F  W  G  W  C  E  Z  W  K  L  K  C  R  E  K  H
E  Z  P  Y  O  I  R  I  R  U  A  Z  N  V  U  J  S  S
V  A  B  R  R  E  Z  N  S  A  W  T  O  O  T  H  F  E
I  A  H  X  T  J  K  D  X  Z  H  X  P  H  N  H  A  O
B  T  L  I  Q  T  J  D  E  T  T  U  B  B  U  A  G  G
C  H  M  T  O  P  R  Y  P  I  H  S  D  N  E  I  R  F
```

☐ ☐ ☐ ☐ ☐ ☐ ☐ **7 quilt sizes**

☐ ☐ ☐ ☐ **4 star blocks**

☐ ☐ ☐ **3 layers in the quilt sandwich**

☐ ☐ **2 borders**

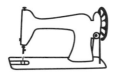

✦ Word RoundUp 2

QUILTING CONCERNS

```
V  S  V  B  Z  W  B  B  V  S  S  R  E  H  T  O  R  B
O  I  Z  S  B  L  A  N  K  E  T  S  T  I  T  C  H  N
X  Z  W  H  I  T  E  P  O  S  S  Y  D  Q  Z  Q  E  C
F  Y  X  F  M  A  E  C  C  I  R  C  L  E  A  E  S  F
R  Z  M  I  K  S  I  Y  M  B  C  Z  N  P  D  P  U  Y
N  Z  U  T  V  W  A  E  A  Z  T  P  F  L  Q  S  S  X
M  O  R  F  S  W  H  R  P  U  U  R  E  R  I  K  E  W
Q  A  R  S  R  C  U  W  Q  U  E  T  I  B  K  X  M  A
M  C  E  O  R  N  Q  Y  B  G  U  L  L  K  H  P  O  C
E  R  L  A  O  E  V  U  N  R  Z  E  I  T  K  S  N  V
P  O  T  R  W  Y  V  I  N  G  E  L  U  K  D  U  A  B
C  S  I  B  E  E  S  W  H  B  E  R  N  I  N  A  J  W
```

☐ ☐ ☐ ☐ ☐ **5 sewing machine brands**

☐ ☐ ☐ ☐ **4 actions to prepare fabric**

☐ ☐ ☐ **3 types of appliqué**

☐ ☐ **2 words for quilters in a group**

☐ **1 fabric family**

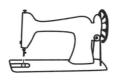

✦ Quilt Block Word Mine 1

See how many words you can make out of the letters in popular quilt blocks!

QUILT BLOCK — S H O O F L Y

5-letter words (3)	4-letter words (8)	3-letter words (10)	2-letter words (9)
_ _ _ _ _	_ _ _ _	_ _ _	_ _
_ _ _ _ _	_ _ _ _	_ _ _	_ _
_ _ _ _ _	_ _ _ _	_ _ _	_ _
	_ _ _ _	_ _ _	_ _
	_ _ _ _	_ _ _	_ _
	_ _ _ _	_ _ _	_ _
	_ _ _ _	_ _ _	_ _
	_ _ _ _	_ _ _	_ _
		_ _ _	_ _
		_ _ _	

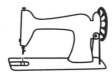

Quilt Block Word Mine 2

See how many words you can make out of the letters in popular quilt blocks!

QUILT BLOCK

6-letter word (1)

— — — — — —

5-letter words (6)

4-letter words (22)

3-letter words (25)

2-letter words (8)

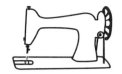

Word Search 1

Quilt Inspiration

```
B  W  I  H  Z  S  O  C  B  E  U  X  H  T  W  J  B  B  M  S
R  O  O  F  F  H  E  L  M  E  H  P  A  R  G  O  T  O  H  P
O  F  O  R  Y  O  J  A  E  E  Q  C  P  V  R  B  Q  O  D  D
O  R  X  K  K  W  D  S  B  C  P  G  G  G  N  I  W  A  R  D
L  I  G  E  T  S  V  S  C  O  N  V  Q  Z  I  A  J  Z  S  S
F  E  Z  N  Q  P  H  S  E  I  R  E  S  N  N  G  K  H  S  T
E  N  P  I  I  E  M  O  C  L  Z  V  R  D  R  O  R  G  G  H
L  D  Q  Z  S  T  H  G  P  I  H  P  T  E  J  E  P  B  E  O
I  B  O  A  F  C  N  Q  X  P  R  E  P  P  F  L  T  K  N  L
T  T  U  G  N  I  S  I  Z  I  L  B  R  L  W  N  G  T  L  B
I  A  N  A  T  U  R  E  A  L  N  C  A  H  J  S  O  K  A  Q
Y  J  E  M  S  U  C  B  R  P  T  B  O  F  L  L  E  C  I  P
```

BOOK	MAGAZINE	SHOW
CLASS	NATURE	SHOW-AND-TELL
CONFERENCE	PAINTING	TILE FLOOR
DRAWING	PATTERN	WORKSHOP
FABRIC	PHOTOGRAPH	
FRIEND	SERIES	

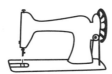

♥ **Crossword Puzzle 4**

ACROSS

1 type of quilt using lots of 1″ squares (2 wds)

7 difficult circular pattern with lots of fine points (2 wds)

10 no more than 24″ in width or length

11 quilts in the Esprit collection

12 outside-of-the-box quilts

14 fabric painting

16 floral sampler from Maryland (2 wds)

21 like fine wine of a certain age

23 selvage quilts are often this type

24 black bias tape plays a large role in this type of quilt (2 wds)

25 graduation memory quilts are often made of this

26 paper makes perfect (2 wds)

DOWN

1 includes fabric photos

2 needle turn and fusible are types of this

3 if Pippi Longstocking had her hair done in Paris (2 wds)

4 no fabric is wrong for this kind of quilt

5 one piece many, many times over

6 familiar and steeped in history

7 contemporary

8 225 patterns/1 quilt (2 wds)

9 held together with evenly spaced yarn knots

13 single solid-color fabric

15 in-"stitch"-tutionalized quilts?

17 100+ years old

18 coffee-cup mat (2 wds)

19 circular, square, and rectangular elements

20 beginner class project

22 a jelly roll race is one of these

21

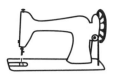

♥ Crossword Puzzle 5

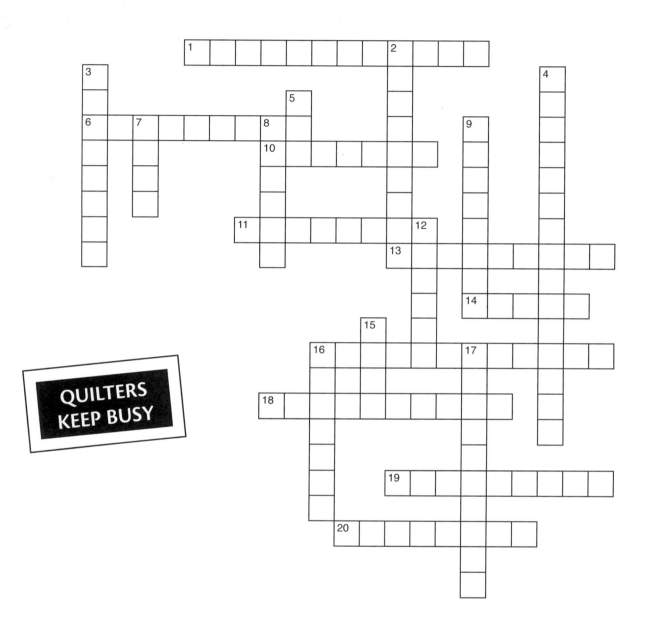

QUILTERS KEEP BUSY

ACROSS

1 a nonprofit that makes blankets for needy kids (2 wds)

6 artist in _____

10 just you and your sewing machine on vacation

11 quilters' camp near Monterey, California

13 breaks out from the guild at large (2 wds)

14 group of like-minded quilt people

16 group of gals that meet with regularity (2 wds)

18 all-hands-on-deck quilt (2 wds)

19 trading pieces (2 wds)

20 periodical

DOWN

2 online photo album for quilt pics

3 technique classroom

4 fat-quarter hoarder (2 wds)

5 a club of queens

7 annual culmination of guild activities

8 take your machine out on the waves

9 retail therapy

12 the blue one is best

15 trade

16 to see how many fabric stores you can visit in a day (2 wds)

17 gathering

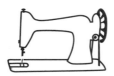

♦ Crossword Puzzle 6

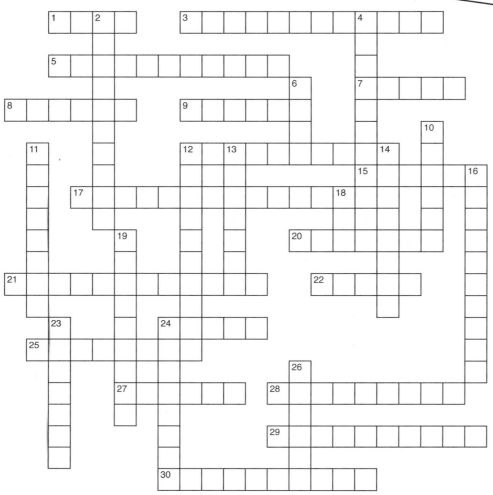

ACROSS

bias, binding (e.g.)

rainbow writing sticks (2 wds)

a repurposed hair clasp (2 wds)

teachers and quilters use this to make a mark

tracing paper

if only sewing machines had one

2 tabletop protector (2 wds)

5 fine filament

17 makes paper piecing super easy (2 wds)

20 needed for a rotary cutter accident

21 shiny on one side, plain on the other (2 wds)

22 queen of all she surveys?

24 cutting device for stray threads

25 pattern made from tin, cardboard, paper, or plastic

27 to keep your fabric stiff

28 curved, straight, and coil-less (e.g.)

29 tool to keep a quilter humble (2 wds)

30 grid or plan out a quilt on this (2 wds)

DOWN

2 sewing room tomato?

4 a quilter's favorite nourishment

6 it blows off some steam?

10 has an eye and comes to a point

11 "Don't touch my fabric _____!"

12 sewing tool necklace

13 finger protector

14 guide your thread through the eye of this helpful tool

16 a place to put your art in progress (2 wds)

18 angels' dance floor

19 the setting on your iron you want when piecing

23 lotion for thread

24 how to set acid dyes

26 memory catcher

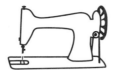

✦ Logic Puzzle 3

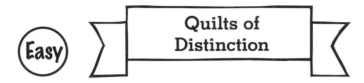

(Easy)

Quilts of Distinction

Michelle Jacobs, a renown quilt collector, has scored a big haul at a quilt auction, winning five award-winning quilts, each by a different famous quilt artist. Using only the clues below, match each quilt to its quilter and the year in which it was created.

1. Jane Hall's quilt was created 24 years before *Purple Treasure.*

2. *Symphony* was quilted 24 years after Harriet Hargrave's masterpiece.

3. Becky Goldsmith's wallhanging was appliquéd in 2007.

4. Kathy Doughty's work is *Purple Treasure.*

5. Harriet Hargrave's piece is either the 1991 piece or *Churn Dash Memories.*

6. Jane Hall's quilt isn't *Stars in the Morning.*

		QUILTERS					QUILTS				
		Becky Goldsmith	Harriet Hargrave	Jane Hall	Alex Anderson	Kathy Doughty	Symphony	Stars in the Morning	Purple Treasure	Polka Dot Parade	Churn Dash Memories
YEARS	1983										
	1991										
	1999										
	2007										
	2015										
QUILTS	Symphony										
	Stars in the Morning										
	Purple Treasure										
	Polka Dot Parade										
	Churn Dash Memories										

YEARS	QUILTERS	QUILTS
1983		
1991		
1999		
2007		
2015		

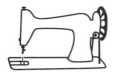

❋ Logic Puzzle 4

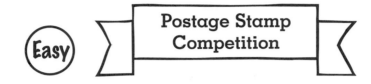

(Easy) Postage Stamp Competition

It's time for the Pacific International Quilt Show's hotly contested competition for the best postage stamp quilt. Using only the clues below, match each quilter to her guild, the total number of patches her quilt contains, and the place her quilt reached in the judging.

1. The person who used 5,184 pieces, the Lighthouse Quilter, and Lynn are three different competitors.

2. The person awarded the viewer's choice ribbon is either the Heritage Quilter or Zinnia.

3. The person awarded second place, the Full Moon Stitcher, and Lynn are three different competitors.

4. The South Bay Sewist is either Tristan or the contestant who used an amazing 9,216 patches.

5. Theresa didn't use 9,216 patches.

6. Of the person who used 8,064 patches and the quilter who used 9,216 patches, one is Lynn and the other is the South Bay Sewist.

7. The quilter who won first place represents the Lighthouse Quilters.

8. Tristan is from the Full Moon Stitchers.

		QUILTERS				GUILDS				PRIZES			
		Theresa	Lynn	Tristan	Zinnia	Full Moon Stitchers	Lighthouse Quilters	Heritage Quilters	South Bay Sewists	First	Second	Third	Viewer's choice
PIECES	4,320												
	5,184												
	8,064												
	9,216												
PRIZES	First												
	Second												
	Third												
	Viewer's choice												
GUILD	Full Moon Stitchers												
	Lighthouse Quilters												
	Heritage Quilters												
	South Bay Sewists												

PIECES	QUILTERS	GUILDS	PRIZES
4,320			
5,184			
8,064			
9,216			

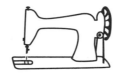

Word Scramble 3

Unscramble the words to find popular quilting terms.

NOTIONS
AND TOOLS
GALORE

PSNI — — — —

NCISUIPNHO — — — — — — — — —

LKHCA EAKRMR — — — — — — — — — —

OISRCSSS — — — — — — — —

WSBEXAE — — — — — — —

ENLEED — — — — — —

ERRLU — — — — —

AMFINIEGR — — — — — — — — —

TPEA ESAMUER — — — — — — — — — —

EMAS PEIPRR — — — — — — — — —

HDETEARR — — — — — — — —

IBHTMEL — — — — — — —

TESTTIOL — — — — — — — —

VGOLSE — — — — — —

KPGNINI RHAESS — — — — — — — — — — — —

WISEGN EGAGU — — — — — — — — — —

ONDEWR ILCP — — — — — — — — —

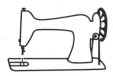

Word Scramble 4

Unscramble the words to find popular quilting terms.

COLOR PLAY

CAID ERGNE _ _ _ _   _ _ _ _ _ _

ABYB BEUL _ _ _ _   _ _ _ _

RAMEB _ _ _ _ _ _

LEDOANC _ _ _ _ _ _ _

BKICR RDE _ _ _ _ _ _   _ _ _

TCAERHSREU _ _ _ _ _ _ _ _ _ _ _

EBLBUB MGU _ _ _ _ _ _   _ _ _ _

EFIR-NEENGI DER _ _ _ _ _ ' _ _ _ _ _ _   _ _ _

TGPLAENG _ _ _ _ _ _ _ _

ARAMTAHN _ _ _ _ _ _ _ _ _

ICSERE _ _ _ _ _ _ _

IMTN _ _ _ _

CAITPRO _ _ _ _ _ _ _ _

ONLME _ _ _ _ _ _

EBUL _ _ _ _

ACETD ULEB _ _ _ _ _   _ _ _ _

HCSFUAI _ _ _ _ _ _ _ _

OGDRLDNEO _ _ _ _ _ _ _ _ _ _

NBRA RDE _ _ _ _   _ _ _ _

DMIITHGN EBUL _ _ _ _ _ _ _ _   _ _ _ _

ILRCECTE LEUB _ _ _ _ _ _ _ _ _   _ _ _ _

EAVLENDR _ _ _ _ _ _ _ _

LBCAK _ _ _ _ _ _

RPSIGN EGERN _ _ _ _ _ _   _ _ _ _ _

TUGMNALE _ _ _ _ _ _ _ _

MOTOTA RDE _ _ _ _ _ _   _ _ _

RTUS _ _ _ _

NAEGOR _ _ _ _ _ _ _

WEPINRILEK _ _ _ _ _ _ _ _ _ _ _

TALE _ _ _ _ _

IENW _ _ _ _

ITOVEL _ _ _ _ _ _ _

CAHPE _ _ _ _ _ _

COHER _ _ _ _ _ _

DALMEER EGERN _ _ _ _ _ _ _   _ _ _ _ _

LPUM _ _ _ _

NMOROA _ _ _ _ _ _

SAH ARYG _ _ _   _ _ _ _

PALEP _ _ _ _ _

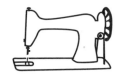

Criss Cross 3

SEWING
MACHINE
FEET

11 letters
QUARTER INCH

10 letters
BUTTONHOLE

FREE MOTION

9 letters
GATHERING

8 letters
APPLIQUÉ

BIAS TAPE

BLIND HEM

BRAIDING

OVERCAST

OVERLOCK

7 letters
CORDING

DARNING

JOINING

OPEN TOE

PRESSER

WALKING

6 letters
FRINGE

NARROW

ROLLER

ZIGZAG

ZIPPER

4 letters
LACE

Criss Cross 4

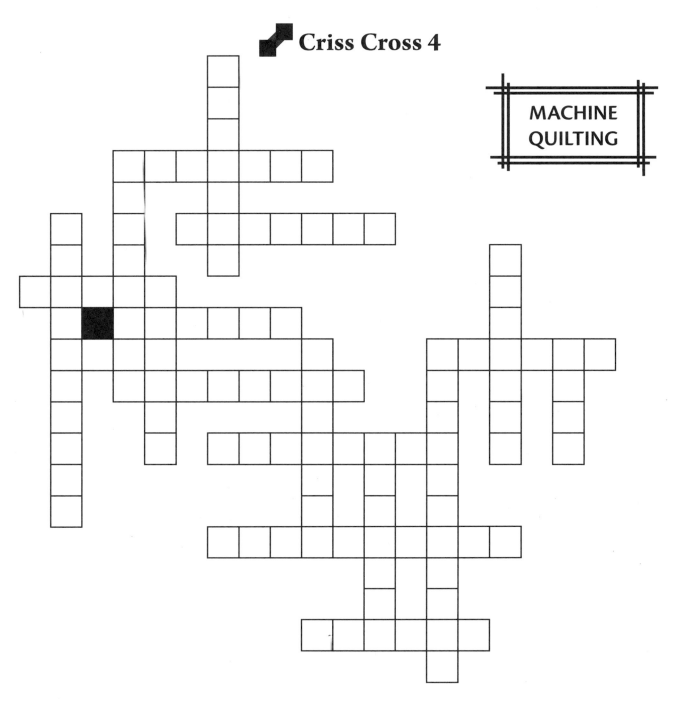

MACHINE
QUILTING

11 letters
DIMENSIONAL

10 letters
FREE MOTION

WHOLECLOTH

8 letters
STRAIGHT

TEMPLATE

TRAPUNTO

7 letters
ALLOVER

FEATHER

MEANDER

STENCIL

STIPPLE

TENSION

6 letters
DESIGN

FLORAL

GLOVES

THREAD

5 letters
MOTIF

4 letters
ECHO

GRID

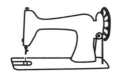

Word RoundUp 3

FABRIC FANTASIES

```
T  W  P  P  S  U  R  E  T  T  U  C  Y  R  A  T  O  R
A  C  I  Q  Z  W  E  D  D  I  N  G  R  I  N  G  M  G
I  U  L  N  X  H  T  A  P  S  D  R  A  K  N  U  R  D
S  X  L  A  D  Q  R  E  P  E  A  T  D  B  R  A  B  S
F  E  T  E  S  I  H  N  Z  A  P  K  N  H  I  W  C  B
R  R  L  E  R  S  N  A  F  R  L  K  M  N  C  I  P  F
B  E  D  V  D  E  N  G  N  N  A  H  X  C  S  A  O  C
O  D  S  R  A  O  H  D  W  D  W  L  K  S  F  M  O  B
L  S  K  Z  M  G  Y  A  N  A  Z  K  O  K  S  A  I  B
T  S  O  Z  Y  H  E  Q  D  I  Y  R  O  G  R  D  R  D
R  J  P  O  H  S  K  R  O  W  S  S  H  S  P  I  N  S
X  D  R  A  P  E  R  E  P  P  I  R  R  T  I  E  O  T
```

☐ ☐ ☐ ☐ ☐ ☐ ☐ **7 fabric terms**

☐ ☐ ☐ ☐ **4 cutting tools**

☐ ☐ ☐ **3 blocks with curved piecing**

☐ ☐ **2 places to learn the ropes**

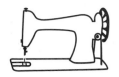

Word RoundUp 4

SUPPLY SAFARI

```
O W O O L Q K S O S O C N O T T O C
W S D D R V Q E V S H O N S T A O C
N U A V O I L E A V R O I R E P U S
N O R C O M P L E M E N T A R Y M N
X G D U A G A X H G O A K W Y W U O
N L X S Y T S T F R F P C I R B A F
E A M K L A W N Q O E G N I T T A B
N N D I F F U Y R Y V H R T Q U H E
I A M O N O C H R O M A T I C Z U Z
L R C W A Z Q H L V J H I A T O F U
W M B X C R P T T H R E A D E P C A
E T F T T R I A D I C S I U P F D G
```

☐ ☐ ☐ ☐ ☐ ☐ **6 fabric types**

☐ ☐ ☐ ☐ **4 color pairings**

☐ ☐ ☐ **3 supplies**

☐ ☐ **2 thread companies**

☐ **1 popular quilting motif**

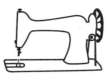

♥ Crossword Puzzle 7

FABRIC TYPE

ACROSS

5   all-natural

7   ewe's uniform?

8   to sew or mow?

9   think lumberjack

12   fuzzy robes and 1950s bedspreads

14   shiny tablecloth

15   so very, very soft

16   man-made material

17   great for sweatshirts or sheep coats

19   a stretch knit fabric

20   100% is best

21   Levi Strauss made this fabric famous

22   woven plaid

24   loom from Lyon

25   flexible and waterproof

DOWN

1   Dorothy from Kansas wore it

2   cloth made from flax

3   barnyard bedhead? (2 wds)

4   semitransparent fabric made of natural fibers

6   cats and cottons

10   comes from worms

11   good for I spy quilts

13   typically comes in 54" or 60" wide (2 wds)

18   early flour industry packaging (2 wds)

23   fabric design made with wax resist

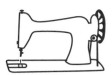

♥ Crossword Puzzle 8

ACROSS

2 _____ pie

5 Naval "block(ade)"? (2 wds)

8 woman of the water (4 wds)

10 Cherry, Fruit, Grandmother's, and May (e.g.)

11 when a crazy quilter has to decide whether to go to the fabric or bead store first (2 wds)

13 also known as Cross and Crown (2 wds)

14 also known as Robbing Peter to Pay Paul (2 wds)

16 child's toy that spins when blown

18 holding a swallow (4 wds)

19 shape of a V

20 like ice cream, you can have a single, double, or triple (2 wds)

22 Paradise, Temperance, and Evergreen are all these types of blocks

23 quilter's tic-tac-toe board (2 wds)

24 blocks with an intended error

DOWN

1 teddy's toes? (2 wds)

2 also known as Double Nine-Patch (3 wds)

3 also known as Wild Goose Chase (3 wds)

4 single-tiered tray for a birthday treat (2 wds)

6 gastropods path? (2 wds)

7 "whoops!" baby blocks (2 wds)

9 gathered circles of fun (2 wds)

12 Abe's assemblage? (2 wds)

14 marriage motif (2 wds)

15 field for summer's pastime

17 butter beater? (2 wds)

18 a formal-wear block (2 wds)

21 Mountain, Carolina, Fire, and Prairie (e.g.)

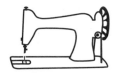

❧ Quilt Block Word Mine 3

See how many words you can make out of the letters in popular quilt blocks!

QUILT BLOCK

ALBUM

4-letter words (5)

— — — —

— — — —

— — — —

— — — —

— — — —

3-letter words (7)

— — —

— — —

— — —

— — —

— — —

— — —

— — —

2-letter words (6)

— —

— —

— —

— —

— —

— —

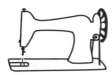

Quilt Block Word Mine 4

See how many words you can make out of the letters in popular quilt blocks!

QUILT BLOCK — JEWEL BOX

5-letter words (5)	4-letter words (6)	3-letter words (20)	2-letter words (6)
_ _ _ _ _	_ _ _ _	_ _ _	_ _
_ _ _ _ _	_ _ _ _	_ _ _	_ _
_ _ _ _ _	_ _ _ _	_ _ _	_ _
_ _ _ _ _	_ _ _ _	_ _ _	_ _
_ _ _ _ _	_ _ _ _	_ _ _	_ _
	_ _ _ _	_ _ _	_ _
		_ _ _	
		_ _ _	
		_ _ _	
		_ _ _	
		_ _ _	
		_ _ _	
		_ _ _	
		_ _ _	
		_ _ _	
		_ _ _	
		_ _ _	
		_ _ _	
		_ _ _	
		_ _ _	

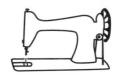

Word Search 2

Fiber and Needle Arts

```
C  H  Q  U  I  L  T  I  N  G  V  E  R  E  B  I  F  C  M  V
K  Q  P  V  Y  D  C  R  O  S  S  S  T  I  T  C  H  Y  V  I
H  K  I  N  B  X  T  B  F  K  U  D  U  W  O  B  C  J  E  S
M  N  N  W  Y  I  U  T  F  G  Y  R  E  D  I  O  R  B  M  E
I  I  U  V  W  C  A  P  P  L  I  Q  U  E  A  P  T  N  N  L
E  T  W  I  L  M  W  A  M  A  C  B  M  Y  M  E  S  H  U  D
S  T  E  R  H  L  Z  F  H  E  A  E  O  S  X  E  K  C  N  C
X  I  D  R  Y  A  Q  K  C  I  W  M  G  R  Q  X  E  M  G  R
U  N  J  E  H  K  Q  A  D  Y  D  C  M  P  C  T  J  X  A  O
E  G  J  A  R  D  L  E  R  R  N  G  R  G  F  I  Q  L  N  C
T  D  B  J  M  E  M  T  Y  S  N  N  Q  I  N  G  R  N  R  H
M  Y  Q  Q  L  D  S  H  P  I  X  T  T  V  H  I  W  B  K  E
Z  C  N  D  E  E  B  G  T  W  N  C  D  B  C  Z  V  G  A  T
L  B  E  X  P  I  Z  T  H  H  X  X  H  C  C  N  T  A  V  F
G  E  I  A  I  F  A  R  Z  T  N  I  O  P  E  L  D  E  E  N
N  M  T  H  W  T  L  B  E  A  D  I  N  G  J  G  S  X  A  W
```

APPLIQUÉ

BEADING

CROCHET

CROSS-STITCH

EMBROIDERY

FABRIC

FIBER

KNITTING

LUCET

MIXED MEDIA

NEEDLE LACE

NEEDLEPOINT

QUILTING

TAPESTRY

TATTING

WEAVING

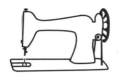

❧ Word Search 3

To Dye For

```
K C Z S S M A D D E R Q H N B D I V C P
O G O X H P T H T G K M R E Y D D I C A
O C F L U I N N P Q M S V O J O R Q Z D
L L O K O W B V M O M F G N I H C T A B
A K O L G R I O R A V Q Y S I H S A R A
I C P P O N W D R M X D L A L O A K W S
D Z L E E R A A G I N W P Y A R G X D Z
K K E G P N F O S A D O H I A M A E T S
M Q A P T H G A B H B N S Y N M O G R E
H R L W W G D R S R H N O I S R E M M I
S S T Z S O E A T T I E D Y E J I P M I
E V G P G B A B A S X M N O G M M R N N
F U V I B D G B J K I D A C S G G O X K
K J D U O Y E K U Q T S E V I T C A E R
U N R S Q Y Y V E P F C E T N E M G I P
I O D Z D R S O Y W A X X R I V V R G I
```

ACID DYE

ARASHI

BATCHING

COLOR WASH

COLORFAST

DYEBATH

IMMERSION

INDIGO

INK

KOOL-AID

MADDER

MORDANT

PIGMENT

REACTIVE

RESIST

RUBBER BAND

SHIBORI

SODA ASH

SOY WAX

STEAM

TIE-DYE

VINEGAR

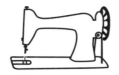

✖ Word RoundUp 5

TEMPTING TERMINOLOGY

```
F  I  N  X  D  V  M  Y  N  O  I  T  O  M  E  E  R  F
U  N  H  B  D  A  A  O  Z  X  Y  S  Z  B  J  S  O  M
W  T  D  B  V  R  E  C  A  R  K  T  N  W  T  U  T  E
B  H  C  I  D  D  S  Q  E  V  R  K  O  I  N  J  C  E
H  E  R  E  P  A  P  T  R  T  X  S  P  D  T  H  U  J
Q  D  L  K  D  F  R  F  D  G  J  P  A  F  O  N  C  G
M  I  J  Z  E  A  E  K  J  N  L  T  I  R  T  F  I  B
J  T  K  B  U  E  D  Y  N  E  I  F  E  I  V  F  R  T
N  C  U  Q  D  V  N  S  J  O  X  E  P  E  T  V  F  K
Y  H  T  A  J  A  A  M  N  R  O  T  N  U  P  A  R  T
X  A  H  W  Y  Q  E  N  N  E  S  O  G  I  N  C  H  U
F  S  H  H  U  E  M  T  U  K  T  P  G  N  I  S  U  F
```

☐ ☐ ☐ ☐ ☐ ☐ **6 quilting types**

☐ ☐ ☐ ☐ **4 color terms**

☐ ☐ ☐ **3 common measurements**

☐ ☐ **2 terms for sewing onto something (e.g., _____ piecing)**

☐ **1 form of gluing fabric**

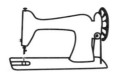

Word RoundUp 6

BEYOND BASICS

```
O  V  E  R  L  O  C  K  A  Z  T  D  M  R  A  D  I  M
S  V  O  V  V  O  B  Q  A  N  Y  P  J  Y  Z  A  L  M
Q  L  L  A  Y  E  R  C  A  K  E  Y  B  W  G  L  A  Z
U  P  O  T  L  T  Z  Y  L  L  W  A  K  T  O  P  B  A
A  R  W  Y  G  C  T  L  C  C  S  Y  R  N  L  H  L  X
R  C  O  L  D  R  O  H  I  T  V  E  G  E  X  B  O  G
E  V  B  D  E  R  T  T  E  E  V  A  L  V  W  X  Y  I
U  Y  A  E  Y  Y  S  X  N  O  R  E  X  M  M  R  A  W
P  P  F  L  L  E  U  H  N  M  A  S  C  A  I  W  Y  I
A  R  L  I  M  S  F  R  O  F  P  Z  T  J  I  B  G  X
E  E  L  O  P  K  U  E  R  A  U  Q  S  M  R  A  H  C
J  Z  D  V  K  T  X  T  T  F  P  V  R  E  G  R  E  S
```

☐ ☐ ☐ ☐ ☐ **5 sewing machine types**

☐ ☐ ☐ ☐ **4 precuts**

☐ ☐ ☐ **3 quilt blocks from nature**

☐ ☐ **2 pre-binding tasks**

☐ ☐ **2 color temperatures**

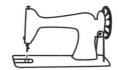

✳ Logic Puzzle 5

Intermediate

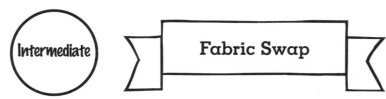

Fabric Swap

The Quilt Guild of Greater Walnut Creek held a fat-quarter exchange last week. Using only the clues that follow, match each quilter to the number of fat quarters she swapped and the fabric color she was swapping for.

1. Ruthmary swapped 6 fat quarters.

2. The quilter who was trading in for yellow was either Ruthmary or Jennifer.

3. The quilter who brought 4 fat quarters to the exchange was looking for green fabric.

4. Amy swapped slightly more fat quarters than the quilter who was searching for grays.

5. Of Jennifer and the quilter who wanted white fabric, one traded 9 fat quarters and the other swapped 4.

		Quilters				Colors			
		Ruthmary	Amy	Jennifer	Deirdre	Gray	Green	White	Yellow
Fat quarters	4								
	6								
	8								
	9								
Colors	Gray								
	Green								
	White								
	Yellow								

Fat quarters	Quilters	Colors
4		
6		
8		
9		

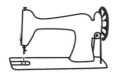

✴ Logic Puzzle 6

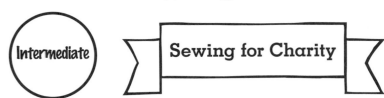

Intermediate

Sewing for Charity

Four quilters from the Bunko and Quilts quilt group are making projects for charity. Using only the clues below, match each quilter to the item she is sewing, determine how many of the items she has made, and figure out what town she lives in.

1. Of the quilters who made 8 items and the friend who made walker caddies, one is Lucy and the other is Alice.

2. The quilter who lives in Laurel made more than the person who lives in Montclair.

3. The sewist who made 2 items made personal care kits for the homeless shelter.

4. Lucy didn't make the pillowcases.

5. Mai made 2 fewer tems than Betsy.

6. The quilter who lives in Oakmore made 2 more items than the quilter who made personal care kits.

7. The quilter who lives in Fruitvale made 4 items more than the quilter who made baby quilts.

		Quilters				Donations				Towns			
		Alice	Betsy	Mai	Lucy	Pillowcases	Baby quilts	Walker caddies	Personal care kits	Fruitvale	Oakmore	Montclair	Laurel
Number of items	2												
	4												
	6												
	8												
Towns	Fruitvale												
	Oakmore												
	Montclair												
	Laurel												
Donations	Pillowcases												
	Baby quilts												
	Walker caddies												
	Personal care kits												

Number of items	Quilters	Donations	Towns
2			
4			
6			
8			

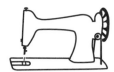

♥ **Crossword Puzzle 9**

BEST IN SHOW

ACROSS

4 vote on this ...

5 people's pick (2 wds)

7 merchants

8 what docents wear (2 wds)

11 listing of classes

13 top honors (3 wds)

14 class costs

16 this modern quilt show used to happen every two years and now occurs yearly

DOWN

1 the National Quilt Museum is located here

2 personal paper identifiers (2 wds)

3 where sustenance can be found

6 artist in _____

9 quilt show

10 where fall Quilt Market is held every year

12 the wheels on this vehicle go round and round

15 critical review

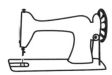

♥ Crossword Puzzle 10

QUILTING TERMS

ACROSS

3 curvy, random, and continuous

4 a sewing tack

6 every square inch

9 the first stitch in any seam

11 follow along

13 lotion for thread

15 "handy" tools? (2 wds)

16 another way to hold it together

17 also known as tacking

18 an antebellum type of skirt

19 scatter, panel, overall, feather (e.g.)

20 a tailor's dance inspired by Chubby Checker? (2 wds)

DOWN

1 moving at will (2 wds)

2 grid lines

5 bird's coat

7 a technique in which you stuff small sections

8 repeat outline stitching (2 wds)

9 slow stitchers quilt this way (2 wds)

10 also known as wadding

12 all one piece

14 use this batting to keep you extra warm

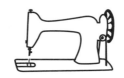

Criss Cross 5

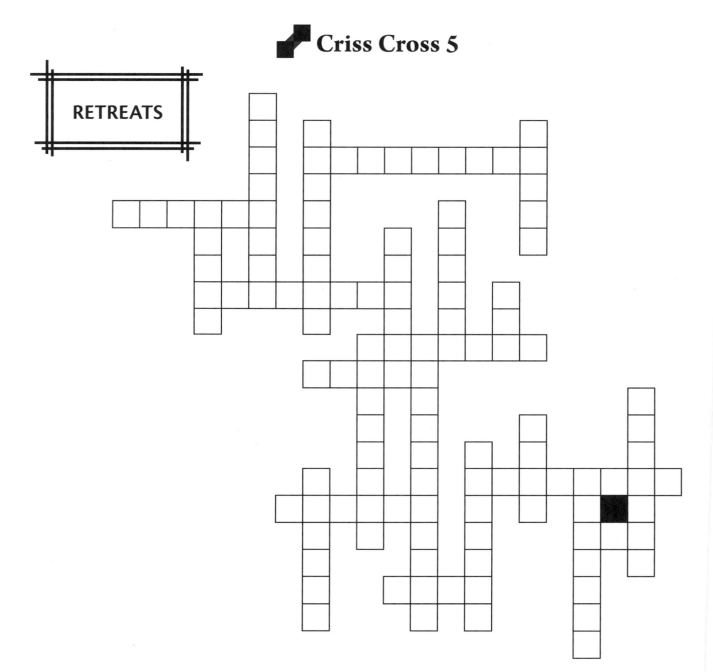

RETREATS

11 letters
DESTINATION

9 letters
CHOCOLATE

8 letters
LAUGHTER

ROOMMATE

SCHEDULE

SUPPLIES

WORKSHOP

7 letters
FRIENDS

LECTURE

LODGING

MACHINE

6 letters
CAMERA

FABRIC

LESSON

SEWING

SNACKS

5 letters
CLASS

MEALS

PLANE

4 letters
FOOD

SHOW

3 letters
CAR

FUN

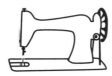

✦ Quilt Block Word Mine 5

See how many words you can make out of the letters in popular quilt blocks!

QUILT BLOCK — B A S K E T

5-letter words (14)	4-letter words (28)	3-letter words (18)	2-letter words (5)
_ _ _ _ _	_ _ _ _	_ _ _	_ _
_ _ _ _ _	_ _ _ _	_ _ _	_ _
_ _ _ _ _	_ _ _ _	_ _ _	_ _
_ _ _ _ _	_ _ _ _	_ _ _	_ _
_ _ _ _ _	_ _ _ _	_ _ _	_ _
_ _ _ _ _	_ _ _ _	_ _ _	
_ _ _ _ _	_ _ _ _	_ _ _	
_ _ _ _ _	_ _ _ _	_ _ _	
_ _ _ _ _	_ _ _ _	_ _ _	
_ _ _ _ _	_ _ _ _	_ _ _	
_ _ _ _ _	_ _ _ _	_ _ _	
_ _ _ _ _	_ _ _ _	_ _ _	
_ _ _ _ _	_ _ _ _	_ _ _	
_ _ _ _ _	_ _ _ _	_ _ _	
	_ _ _ _	_ _ _	
	_ _ _ _	_ _ _	
	_ _ _ _	_ _ _	
	_ _ _ _	_ _ _	
	_ _ _ _		
	_ _ _ _		
	_ _ _ _		
	_ _ _ _		
	_ _ _ _		
	_ _ _ _		
	_ _ _ _		
	_ _ _ _		
	_ _ _ _		
	_ _ _ _		

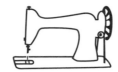

🪡 Word Scramble 5

Unscramble the words to find popular quilting terms.

PTERATN GESIHTW _ _ _ _ _ _ _ _ _ _ _ _ _ _

CFENRH CREVU _ _ _ _ _ _ _ _ _ _ _

RSEAHS _ _ _ _ _ _

KCLHA MRKARE _ _ _ _ _ _ _ _ _ _ _

APTE EMSUAER _ _ _ _ _ _ _ _ _ _ _

TPTREAN _ _ _ _ _ _ _

EGSERR _ _ _ _ _ _

BSUOTTN _ _ _ _ _ _ _

ESALTCI _ _ _ _ _ _ _

AISB PTEA _ _ _ _ _ _ _ _ _

WGSENI EUAGG _ _ _ _ _ _ _ _ _ _ _

PZIREP _ _ _ _ _ _

NTIFACGIERN _ _ _ _ _ _ _ _ _ _ _

HMA _ _ _

INOGNIR ROADB _ _ _ _ _ _ _ _ _ _ _ _

ARINKMG NIPELC _ _ _ _ _ _ _ _ _ _ _ _ _

AGSTTRIH PNIS _ _ _ _ _ _ _ _ _ _ _ _

PNEATTR PRPEA _ _ _ _ _ _ _ _ _ _ _ _

OISNRITUTNCS _ _ _ _ _ _ _ _ _ _ _ _

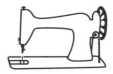

Word Scramble 6

Unscramble the words to find popular quilting terms.

PATTERN PARADISE

VENOLYT _ _ _ _ _ _ _

HCEROVN _ _ _ _ _ _ _

DHOTNSTOHOU _ _ _ _ _ _ _ _ _ _

EGKER KYE _ _ _ _ _   _ _ _

NPAIL _ _ _ _ _

GAMIGNH _ _ _ _ _ _ _

IATK _ _ _ _

ACSANETIOVONLR _ _ _ _ _ _ _ _ _ _ _ _ _

ATNART _ _ _ _ _ _

TSOHWTEESRNU _ _ _ _ _ _ _ _ _ _ _

LSOLCR _ _ _ _ _ _

OILUQTAEFR _ _ _ _ _ _ _ _ _ _

GAOUFLCAEM _ _ _ _ _ _ _ _ _ _

FRELU-ED-SLI _ _ _ _ _ - _ _ - _ _ _

ALEISYP _ _ _ _ _ _ _

YRAGEL _ _ _ _ _ _

HEINORGERBN _ _ _ _ _ _ _ _ _ _ _

LSACE _ _ _ _ _

ITEOL _ _ _ _ _

NEALP _ _ _ _ _

QHNAEURLI _ _ _ _ _ _ _ _ _

ICOMGETER _ _ _ _ _ _ _ _ _

PSITRES _ _ _ _ _ _ _

ROEDRB IPNRT _ _ _ _ _ _   _ _ _ _ _

OKLPA TOD _ _ _ _ _   _ _ _

SEAKEWTEBAV _ _ _ _ _ _ _ _ _ _ _

CARBOED _ _ _ _ _ _ _

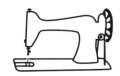

DESIGN
TOOLS

 **Criss Cross 6**

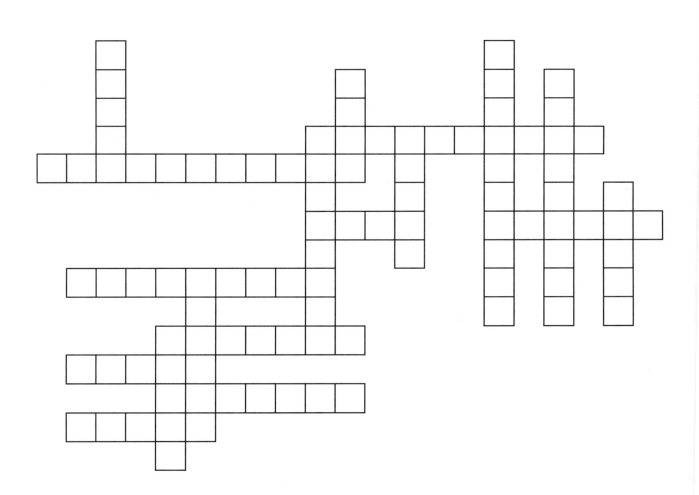

11 letters
INSPIRATION

10 letters
CALCULATOR

CREATIVITY

9 letters
CHOCOLATE

PINTEREST

8 letters
COMPUTER

7 letters
PATTERN

PENCILS

6 letters
ERASER

VELLUM

5 letters
BOOKS

CLASS

IDEAS

MUSIC

PAPER

RULER

4 letters
PENS

PLAN

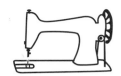

Criss Cross 7

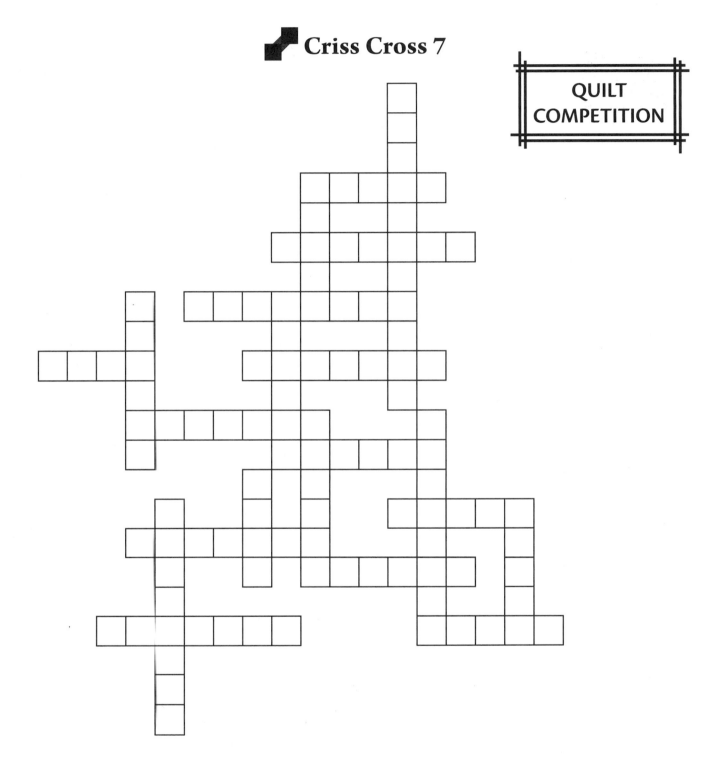

QUILT COMPETITION

11 letters
WALLHANGING

8 letters
NATIONAL
REGIONAL
SHIPPING

7 letters
ENTRIES
LONGARM
MACHINE
RIBBONS
SPONSOR

6 letters
JUDGED
SECOND
SLEEVE
SLIDES
PRIZES

5 letters
FIRST
GROUP
GUILD
LABEL
THEME

4 letters
FAIR
HAND

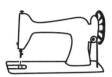

♥ Crossword Puzzle 11

COLOR WHEEL

ACROSS

2 relative lightness and darkness

6 colors next to each other on the wheel

7 mixing two colors to get a third

9 three colors evenly spaced around the color wheel

11 red, yellow, blue (e.g.)

13 colors that are vivid or bold in nature

14 green, orange, purple (e.g.)

15 when you add black

16 practical guide to color mixing (2 wds)

18 yellow-orange, blue-green (e.g.)

19 a color that is calming or soothing in nature

20 colorer

DOWN

1 intensity

3 the rainbow

4 when you add white

5 red and green; blue and orange (e.g.)

8 look through a red lens to see this (2 wds)

10 rainbow circle (i.e., 2 wds)

12 a lens that allows the user see the world in gray scale (2 wds)

17 Roy G. Biv (i.e.)

18 when you add gray

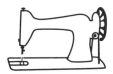

♥ Crossword Puzzle 12

ACROSS

6 proper _____ keeps your stitches even

8 happiness is a full _____

9 manual-operated drive (2 wds)

10 first started selling sewing machines in their wish book in 1894

12 not your sister but your _____

13 hungry pups? (2 wds)

14 a part to create a meandering path (3 wds)

16 extra goodies for your machine

18 first appeared in the 1913 Sears catalog

19 serger's stitch

22 Singer's salve?

23 Singer's stinger?

24 old sewing machine foot pedal

DOWN

1 not domestic or mid-arm

2 Swiss sewing machine company

3 Nancy Sinatra had one inside her boot (2 wds)

4 sewing jewel that comes in a plain black case

5 the first group of sewing machines ever manufactured only did this (2 wds)

7 Isaac _____ (sewing machine inventor)

10 straight-sewing assistant (2 wds)

11 flanged, hopping, free-motion (e.g.)

13 makes your machine go (2 wds)

15 what a needle goes through on a sewing machine (2 wds)

17 number one sewing machine manufacturer in the world

20 Swedish sewing machine company

21 connects the foot pedal

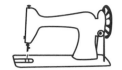

✦ Logic Puzzle 7

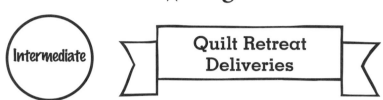

Intermediate

Quilt Retreat Deliveries

Todd and Tony work for Full Bobbins Quilt Retreat. As a luxury quilting retreat, Full Bobbins takes care of all the little details. On arrival day, Todd and Tony have a number of suitcases to deliver to the quilters' rooms. Help them out by matching each bag to its color, weight, guest, and room assignment.

1. The piece that weighs 41 pounds is purple.

2. Of the suitcase that weighs 41 pounds and the black luggage, one is heading to The Victorian bedroom and the other is April's bag.

3. Of the bag that weighs 35 pounds and the purple suitcase, one is going to The Cottage and the other is Kerry's.

4. The bag that weighs 44 pounds isn't plaid.

5. Kerry's suitcase is going to go to Mountain Vista room.

6. Kerry's bag isn't plaid.

7. Stacy's bag isn't supposed to go to The Fireplace Suite.

8. The luggage that needs to go to the Mountain Vista room isn't blue.

9. The luggage that needs to go to The Victorian bedroom weighs 3 pounds more than Kerry's piece.

10. Stacy's suitcase doesn't weigh 44 pounds.

11. Kerry's suitcase weighs 3 pounds less than Gailen's bag.

		Quilters					Colors					Bedrooms				
		Kerry	April	Dina	Gailen	Stacy	Black	Blue	Red	Purple	Plaid	The Ocean View	The Victorian	The Cottage	Mountain Vista	The Fireplace Suite
Weight	35															
	38															
	41															
	44															
	47															
Bedrooms	The Ocean View															
	The Victorian															
	The Cottage															
	Mountain Vista															
	The Fireplace Suite															
Colors	Black															
	Blue															
	Red															
	Purple															
	Plaid															

Weight	Quilters	Colors	Bedrooms
35			
38			
41			
44			
47			

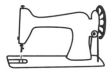

✵ Logic Puzzle 8

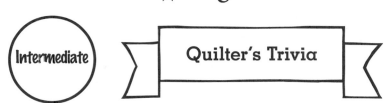

Intermediate

Quilter's Trivia

The On the Mountain Quilter's Guild held a Quilter's Trivia contest at their annual potluck meeting. Using only the clues below, determine each player's final score in the trivia game, the dish she brought for the potluck, and her hometown.

1. The quilter from Martinez didn't bring garlic bread.

2. Miki, the quilter who brought lasagna, and the guild member who brought garlic bread are three different people.

3. The quilter from Pleasant Hill didn't bring the fruit platter.

4. The member from Concord scored 10 points more than Miki at trivia.

5. Dawn scored more points than Miki in trivia.

6. Meredith scored 10 points more than the person from Walnut Creek.

7. The quilter from Walnut Creek didn't bring the fruit platter.

8. Becky didn't bring the fruit platter.

9. Of the quilter from Concord and Jen, one brought jello salad and the other scored 70 points at trivia.

10. Dawn is from Pleasant Hill.

11. The quilter who scored 50 points at trivia isn't from Lafayette.

12. Becky scored 50 points.

		Quilters					Dishes					Towns				
		Jen	Becky	Miki	Dawn	Meredith	Jello salad	Garlic bread	Lasagna	Prune whip	Fruit platter	Martinez	Concord	Pleasant Hill	Walnut Creek	Lafayette
Scores	30															
	40															
	50															
	60															
	70															
Towns	Martinez															
	Concord															
	Pleasant Hill															
	Walnut Creek															
	Lafayette															
Dishes	Jello salad															
	Garlic bread															
	Lasagna															
	Prune whip															
	Fruit platter															

Scores	Quilters	Dishes	Towns
30			
40			
50			
60			
70			

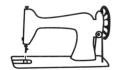

Word RoundUp 7

FABRIC FUN

```
M  K  S  V  S  N  L  A  N  O  I  T  I  D  A  R  T  S
A  I  F  X  S  C  I  S  S  O  R  S  P  T  D  Q  L  D
P  H  N  R  T  T  M  O  G  P  R  I  E  T  Z  Q  R  E
P  T  J  I  V  R  D  S  D  S  N  P  W  L  T  A  N  E
L  O  L  L  A  A  M  W  W  S  U  N  N  D  F  M  K  O
I  L  P  P  G  T  M  J  G  H  S  E  E  T  J  F  Z  Y
Q  C  J  Y  B  E  U  N  J  E  W  T  R  B  A  Q  A  B
U  E  S  W  C  T  R  R  L  B  I  S  B  U  X  K  K  R
E  L  R  I  O  E  G  D  E  X  R  F  D  N  T  R  Q  V
I  O  F  B  D  L  E  T  G  I  N  F  M  W  P  C  V  Y
L  H  K  O  S  E  E  W  W  U  J  D  W  P  I  N  E  W
K  W  M  C  N  A  Q  D  T  R  U  L  E  R  R  L  M  L
```

☐ ☐ ☐ ☐ ☐ ☐   **6 quilt styles**

☐ ☐ ☐ ☐   **4 common tools**

☐ ☐   **2 guild activities**

☐   **1 word for unsew**

☐   **1 word for sketch**

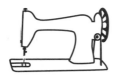

Word RoundUp 8

SEWING STYLE

```
P  L  X  A  G  N  G  Q  V  C  I  M  G  A  Z  G  I  Z
B  N  T  W  N  E  B  H  S  V  L  E  E  H  W  N  I  P
S  H  O  O  F  L  Y  T  S  H  O  S  O  Z  M  J  G  E
R  O  L  O  O  P  S  K  O  O  S  T  A  G  X  Q  L  X
R  U  C  U  T  T  E  R  X  U  T  E  E  T  I  M  O  T
X  M  L  Y  E  K  G  O  F  R  W  H  Q  K  I  D  X  V
H  D  G  E  A  B  G  E  U  G  N  A  G  C  N  N  N  D
O  M  K  W  R  R  W  K  E  L  H  P  P  I  I  A  Z  I
C  O  R  N  A  N  D  B  E  A  N  S  K  R  A  Q  L  P
X  B  R  O  K  E  N  D  I  S  H  E  S  T  A  R  R  B
J  R  E  L  F  S  B  U  V  S  A  S  G  I  A  E  T  J
U  C  H  U  R  N  D  A  S  H  U  N  O  R  H  M  B  S
```

☐ ☐ ☐ ☐ ☐ ☐ ☐ ☐   **8 HST blocks**

☐ ☐ ☐ ☐   **4 stitches**

☐ ☐ ☐   **3 rotary cutting tools**

☐   **1 traditional color**

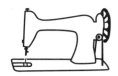

Word Search 4

Art Quilting

```
M  I  S  T  H  R  E  A  D  S  K  E  T  C  H  I  N  G  U  S
O  P  L  A  Y  E  R  I  N  G  U  A  H  S  V  E  I  E  H  Q
Z  Y  J  V  H  V  V  F  T  S  Y  C  N  O  O  Q  M  I  H  S
D  I  M  E  N  S  I  O  N  A  L  O  M  I  R  B  B  M  U  G
M  I  X  E  D  M  E  D  I  A  I  X  J  E  E  O  U  R  T  N
P  B  E  A  D  I  N  G  U  T  E  G  F  L  R  L  F  I  P  I
B  G  N  L  S  L  E  E  A  T  F  S  L  I  T  A  G  N  W  D
P  T  R  L  Y  D  X  S  L  E  N  I  R  E  C  L  H  K  U  L
N  A  D  F  L  X  I  Q  P  A  S  V  X  E  O  A  L  M  Y  O
O  E  I  U  V  H  A  R  H  N  G  D  O  L  M  W  Y  N  F
E  P  R  N  O  V  C  T  I  G  I  E  W  F  L  B  V  F  E  C
O  C  O  R  T  S  O  N  G  N  S  T  P  V  A  S  N  T  H  I
G  Q  P  M  D  T  G  V  A  I  T  K  K  F  G  N  D  T  H  R
L  M  N  N  O  C  X  G  G  E  W  R  I  F  E  K  P  A  Z  B
I  H  A  H  T  T  G  N  I  Y  U  H  X  Z  E  E  M  D  Z  A
F  L  P  Y  K  B  A  U  C  D  Q  H  Y  C  D  S  G  F  N  F
```

BEADING	FABRIC FOLDING	MULTEX
COLLAGE	IMPROVISATION	PAINT
DEPTH	INK	PHOTO TRANSFER
DIMENSIONAL	LANDSCAPE	SHIBORI
DYEING	LAYERING	SURFACE DESIGN
EMBELLISHING	MIXED MEDIA	THREAD SKETCHING

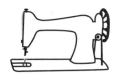

✦ Word Search 5

Things Quilters Sew

```
F  H  M  F  A  B  R  I  C  B  O  W  L  Z  O  U  Q  Q  L  D
A  H  X  N  A  W  R  E  S  R  U  P  A  H  D  O  A  U  E  L
B  D  O  L  L  Q  U  I  L  T  V  R  O  T  Q  S  G  I  L  E
R  N  V  C  U  V  F  K  L  I  P  D  A  Z  Y  O  S  L  J  D
I  N  Y  H  O  D  L  C  B  I  P  O  W  E  L  D  B  T  W  U
C  H  A  I  Z  V  K  T  D  G  A  B  E  G  A  R  O  T  S  L
B  H  V  P  W  V  E  K  X  G  N  I  G  N  A  H  L  L  A  W
A  T  J  Y  K  P  S  R  F  F  I  N  F  V  Q  R  Q  T  G  I
S  O  A  C  Z  I  S  B  L  Z  F  S  B  P  O  O  F  O  K  S
K  L  W  M  V  Y  N  B  B  E  G  V  N  M  L  Z  O  P  L  G
E  C  V  Z  E  M  P  W  L  A  T  C  W  P  I  G  M  P  E  I
T  E  L  M  A  C  O  S  B  M  P  T  S  T  B  X  Z  E  D  F
Z  L  M  H  M  L  A  E  F  B  U  Z  E  H  Y  K  V  R  W  H
I  B  S  C  L  T  T  L  M  E  T  R  I  H  S  T  A  E  W  S
Y  A  T  I  H  O  R  T  P  G  C  L  X  N  E  L  F  F  U  D
S  T  P  A  T  S  W  T  E  K  N  A  L  B  C  I  N  C  I  P
```

COVERLETTE	PILLOW	SWEATSHIRT
DOLL QUILT	PLACE MAT	TABLECLOTH
DUFFLE	POOF	TOPPER
FABRIC BASKET	PURSE	TOTE BAG
FABRIC BOWL	QUILT	WALLHANGING
NAPKIN	SHAM	
PICNIC BLANKET	STORAGE BAG	

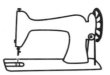

♥ Crossword Puzzle 13

BLOCKS 2

ACROSS

2   also known as Arkansas Troubles (2 wds)

5   2 × 2 squares (2 wds)

6   where quilt national is held (2 wds)

9   also known as Cathedral Windows (2 wds)

12   it turns bright red in fall (2 wds)

13   city in the eastern bloc(k)

15   Crown of Thorns (e.g., 3 wds)

17   how we measured time before clocks (2 wds)

18   German dish? (2 wds)

19   shattered china (2 wds)

DOWN

1   the bright and shining general (2 wds)

3   wino's way? (2 wds)

4   you can either ride the _____ or sit on the _____ (2 wds)

7   also known as Gentleman's Fancy (4 wds)

8   problems in the sunflower state (2 wds)

10   south for the winter (2 wds)

11   zigzag twinkler? (2 wds)

14   bumpy street surface

16   the center of a pippin, crispin, or golden delicious (2 wds)

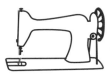

♦ Crossword Puzzle 14

FABRIC TERMS

ACROSS

4 all-natural

5 18″ (2 wds)

6 iron without moving

8 maker's mark?

10 a few feet

11 first run of a new fabric design (2 wds)

13 stretchy

15 yardage sold without a bolt (2 wds)

17 the hand of a fabric

21 a wash of water-based paint tinted with a colored pigment (2 wds)

22 on the 45° angle

23 fabric company version of a "do-over"?

24 personal fabric collection

DOWN

1 man-made material

2 natural red dye from bedstraw plant family

3 a fabric family

7 more than one of the same

9 rag trade center? (2 wds)

12 make laundry origami

14 fusible, sew-in (e.g.)

16 old-time name of fabric stores (2 wds)

18 lengthwise and crosswise (e.g.)

19 yummy leftover

20 ready to use

22 large unit of fabric

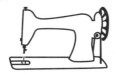

Word Scramble 7

Unscramble the words to find popular quilting terms.

TAN
BY ANY OTHER
NAME ...

LFHES _ _ _ _ _

GIHLT TAPCORI _ _ _ _ _   _ _ _ _ _ _ _

AILVANL _ _ _ _ _ _ _   FBUF _ _ _ _

EISQBU _ _ _ _ _ _   PLAER _ _ _ _ _

GEHLGSEL _ _ _ _ _ _ _ _   HTEWI LCOTEHCOA _ _ _ _ _   _ _ _ _ _ _ _ _ _

EINNL _ _ _ _ _   ANFW _ _ _ _

SONW _ _ _ _   CAMRE _ _ _ _ _

LSASHEEL _ _ _ _ _ _ _ _   RCON LKSI _ _ _ _   _ _ _ _

CURE _ _ _ _   HLITG HKAIK _ _ _ _ _   _ _ _ _ _

NSAD _ _ _ _   EBEIG _ _ _ _ _

EWATH _ _ _ _ _   NBEO _ _ _ _

NLMODA _ _ _ _ _ _   JAVNAO ITHEW _ _ _ _ _ _   _ _ _ _ _

ITBCISU _ _ _ _ _ _   AÉFC UA ILAT _ _ _ _   _ _   _ _ _ _

BLAASTEAR _ _ _ _ _ _ _ _ _   LOMEATA _ _ _ _ _ _ _

ECALM _ _ _ _ _   GCEHAPMAN _ _ _ _ _ _ _ _ _

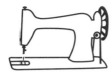

Word Scramble 8

Unscramble the words to find popular quilting terms.

RTSAS ADN SSPETRI _ _ _ _ _ _   _ _ _   _ _ _ _ _ _ _

ABSETK _ _ _ _ _ _ _

HCUNR AHSD _ _ _ _ _ _   _ _ _ _

OIUMRISS SATR _ _ _ _ _ _ _ _   _ _ _ _

YNLMOEE ARST _ _ _ _ _ _ _   _ _ _ _

SWEERBPID _ _ _ _ _ _ _ _ _

RAI TCASEL _ _ _   _ _ _ _ _ _

CJOSBA ADLRDE _ _ _ _ _ _   _ _ _ _ _ _

SIRHI HINAC _ _ _ _ _   _ _ _ _ _

OBNSNUETN USE _ _ _ _ _ _ _ _ _ _   _ _ _

LGO AICNB _ _ _   _ _ _ _ _

RFUO-CPAHT _ _ _ _ _ ' _ _ _ _ _

EBASR WPA _ _ _ _ _ ' _   _ _ _

ABZLGIN ASRT _ _ _ _ _ _ _   _ _ _ _

CILKPE HISD _ _ _ _ _ _   _ _ _ _

EROAGN EPEL _ _ _ _ _ _   _ _ _ _

WNCOR FO TRNHSO _ _ _ _ _   _ _   _ _ _ _ _ _

SKNSAA UBLTOESR _ _ _ _ _ _   _ _ _ _ _ _ _ _

SCORS ADN NCOWR _ _ _ _ _   _ _ _   _ _ _ _ _

HOSUECRTOU SPSET _ _ _ _ _ _ _ _ _   _ _ _ _ _

ORSE FO NASOHR _ _ _ _ _   _ _   _ _ _ _ _ _

TFELSONAGS _ _ _ _ _ _ _ _ _ _

AVAHTEEWERN _ _ _ _ _ _ _ _ _ _ _

OSOEG KRSACT _ _ _ _ _   _ _ _ _ _

OHUR SGSLA _ _ _ _   _ _ _ _ _

OIOH RTSA _ _ _ _   _ _ _ _

HGWI RSEO _ _ _ _   _ _ _ _

IRLA CEFNE _ _ _ _ _   _ _ _ _ _

EYAENK ZPZLEU _ _ _ _ _ _   _ _ _ _ _ _

RMTOS TA SAE _ _ _ _ _   _ _   _ _ _

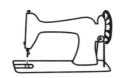

Criss Cross 8

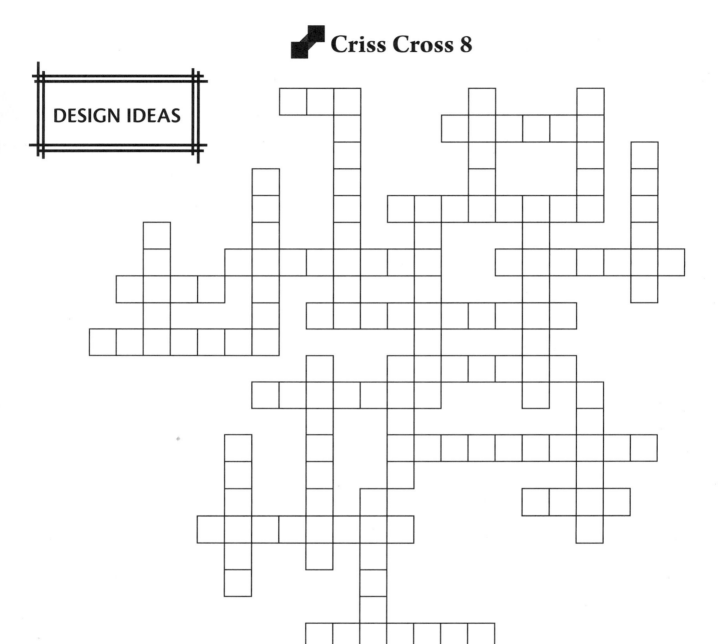

10 letters
EMBROIDERY
WHOLECLOTH

9 letters
EMBELLISH

8 letters
APPLIQUÉ
CRYSTALS
PATTERNS
QUILTING
STRAIGHT
TRAPUNTO

7 letters
BATTING
BINDING
BORDERS
ON POINT
SASHING
SETTING

6 letters
BLOCKS
FABRIC
IMPROV
PIECED
PIPING

5 letters
LABEL
ORDER
PAINT
SCALE

4 letters
SIZE
TIES

3 letters
DYE

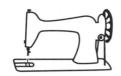

Criss Cross 9

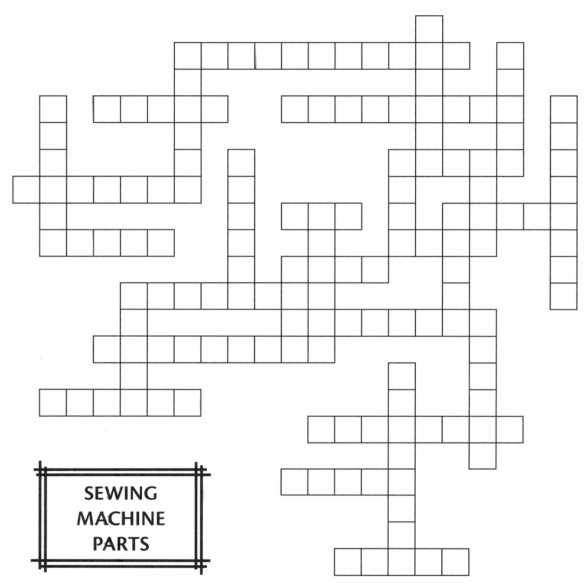

SEWING
MACHINE
PARTS

11 letters	**8 letters**	**6 letters**	**5 letters**	**4 letters**
SHUTTLE HOOK	KNEE LIFT	BOBBIN	GEARS	BELT
9 letters	SET SCREW	LOOPER	KNIFE	CASE
LIGHT BULB	SPOOL CAP	MANUAL	MOTOR	CORD
RACE COVER	SPOOL PIN	SCREWS	PEDAL	FEET
	THREADER	SPRING	PLATE	KNOB
	7 letters	SWITCH	SHAFT	**3 letters**
	FEED DOG	WINDER	SHANK	FLY
			TABLE	
			WHEEL	

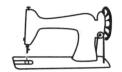

Logic Puzzle 9

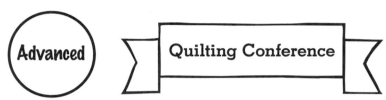

Advanced

Quilting Conference

The Variety in Quilting conference is being held this month, where a different class will be taught each day. Match each teacher to his or her topic, and determine the day on which each will teach a class.

1. Of the curved piecing expert and the person who will teach on August 13, one is Jackie and the other is Tom.

2. Of the person who will speak on August 12 and the person who will teach on August 13, one is Tom and the other is demonstrating improvisational piecing.

3. Sally is scheduled 1 day before Tom.

4. Sally will be either the person who will speak on August 11 or on art quilting.

		Quilters				Classes			
		Sally	Jackie	Tom	Bill	Curved piecing	Improvisational piecing	Art quilting	Quilt drafting
Days	August 11								
	August 12								
	August 13								
	August 14								
Classes	Curved piecing								
	Improvisational piecing								
	Art quilting								
	Quilt drafting								

Days	Quilters	Classes
August 11		
August 12		
August 13		
August 14		

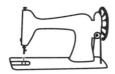

✦ Logic Puzzle 10

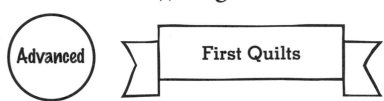

Advanced — First Quilts

The Rapid Stitchers quilt group was chatting at their last get-together, sharing stories of their first quilts. Match each quilter to the year she made her first quilt and what kind of quilt it was.

1. Kiki didn't make a T-shirt quilt.

2. Of Jean and Kiki, one made her first quilt in 1985 and the other made a baby quilt.

3. Of the person who started quilting in 1983 and the person who started in 1987, one made a wallhanging and the other is Alice.

4. The 5 quilters are Kennedy, the quilter who made the T-shirt quilt, the person who started quilting in 1987, the person who made the baby quilt, and the quilter who made her first piece in 1984.

5. The person who made the Star block throw started some time before Jean.

		Quilters					First quilts				
		Cynthia	Kiki	Jean	Kennedy	Alice	Star block throw	T-shirt quilt	Photo quilt	Baby quilt	Wallhanging
Years	1983										
	1984										
	1985										
	1986										
	1987										
First quilts	Star block throw										
	T-shirt quilt										
	Photo quilt										
	Baby quilt										
	Wallhanging										

Years	Quilters	First quilts
1983		
1984		
1985		
1986		
1987		

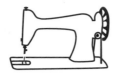

Word RoundUp 9

PATTERN PLAY

```
O  C  B  E  L  Z  Z  U  P  S  N  A  M  H  C  T  U  D
Y  H  A  D  M  Q  V  O  I  M  L  O  S  L  J  X  H  N
Z  A  L  T  D  A  R  N  O  C  H  K  L  E  C  E  I  P
K  R  T  U  O  N  A  C  Z  A  C  A  J  U  M  W  O  W
D  M  I  T  X  Y  Z  T  E  A  E  M  X  H  N  B  I  G
O  K  M  A  J  E  I  Z  R  D  J  K  G  O  C  N  H  Z
M  M  O  I  Z  V  F  T  E  W  R  F  E  N  D  T  W  X
Q  I  R  L  Z  Y  E  R  I  B  X  R  F  B  I  Q  A  J
U  I  E  O  D  S  A  Y  E  R  M  N  L  Q  K  R  A  P
T  Z  B  R  O  U  O  U  T  H  E  O  X  B  Q  A  T  Q
Q  I  X  O  Q  S  C  R  A  P  W  R  E  L  P  M  A  S
E  M  G  S  D  N  O  P  E  H  T  N  I  E  S  O  O  G
```

☐ ☐ ☐ ☐ ☐ **5 Flying Geese blocks**

☐ ☐ ☐ ☐ **4 fix-it techniques**

☐ ☐ ☐ ☐ **4 varied quilt patterns**

☐ ☐ **2 single units**

☐ **1 style of album quilt**

Word RoundUp 10

BEAUTIFUL BASICS

```
N M R Q J M L T S R V E M I N E D Q
U I Q O W I V S P R Q L S R C Y D H
J C N R E N U M J G A C A X X P K P
C E F E N K I M A J D X P S R V M Q
E K R S P Y T O B W N I B A C G O L
R L I S L A M V S H C T A P R U O F
U I E N E L T S P I A B W B I Y B H
T S V I N Y G C F U E L L I N E H C
A W E L N W J E H G P O B X Y V N N
N K E S A N R E D O M G N I D N I B
I X L U L W R F V I E G Q L E B A L
M Y S M F R A I L F E N C E S D O S
```

□ □ □ □ □ □ □ **7 fabric types**

□ □ □ □ **4 basic blocks**

□ □ **2 finishing touches**

□ □ **2 quilt types starting with M**

□ **1 outer edge of the quilt**

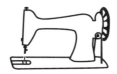

🍂 Quilt Block Word Mine 6

See how many words you can make out of the letters in popular quilt blocks!

QUILT BLOCK

HOUSE

4-letter words (4)

— — — —

— — — —

— — — —

— — — —

3-letter words (7)

— — —

— — —

— — —

— — —

— — —

— — —

— — —

2-letter words (9)

— —

— —

— —

— —

— —

— —

— —

— —

— —

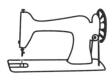

⚜ Quilt Block Word Mine 7

See how many words you can make out of the letters in popular quilt blocks!

QUILT BLOCK — PINE TREE

7-letter words (3)

— — — — — — —
— — — — — — —
— — — — — — —

6-letter words (8)

— — — — — —
— — — — — —
— — — — — —
— — — — — —
— — — — — —
— — — — — —
— — — — — —
— — — — — —

5-letter words (18)

— — — — —
— — — — —
— — — — —
— — — — —
— — — — —
— — — — —
— — — — —
— — — — —
— — — — —
— — — — —
— — — — —
— — — — —
— — — — —
— — — — —
— — — — —
— — — — —
— — — — —
— — — — —

4-letter words (27)

— — — —
— — — —
— — — —
— — — —
— — — —
— — — —
— — — —
— — — —
— — — —
— — — —
— — — —
— — — —
— — — —
— — — —
— — — —
— — — —
— — — —
— — — —
— — — —
— — — —
— — — —
— — — —
— — — —
— — — —
— — — —
— — — —
— — — —

3-letter words (22)

— — —
— — —
— — —
— — —
— — —
— — —
— — —
— — —
— — —
— — —
— — —
— — —
— — —
— — —
— — —
— — —
— — —
— — —
— — —
— — —
— — —
— — —

2-letter words (6)

— —
— —
— —
— —
— —
— —

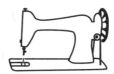

♥ Crossword Puzzle 15

STITCHERY

ACROSS

6 fine filament

7 cross-stitch fabric base

8 Aunt _____ (vintage embroidery transfer company)

10 thread for embroidery

11 anything that uses a needle for construction

13 fiber decorations

15 bringing your needle up and over trim

17 repair your sock

18 type of cross-stitch

19 by hand or machine

20 sewing tool necklace

DOWN

1 embroidery made with yarn in tufts

2 finger protector

3 shiny threads used primarily for needlework (2 wds)

4 to pull thread with a needle

5 cross-stitch piece for beginners

9 squaring up using a frame, heat, or water

11 embroidery and upholstery (e.g.)

12 thread's target

14 embroidery using red thread

15 a hashtag is made with this technique

16 pinochle pattern? (2 wds)

21 for stitching in—not jumping through

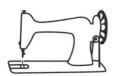

 Crossword Puzzle 16

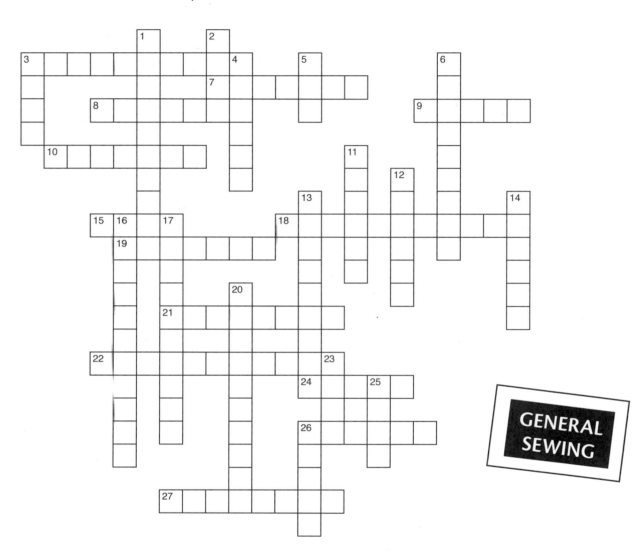

GENERAL SEWING

ACROSS

3 enclosed seam (2 wds)

7 fancy gathering of fabric

8 bits and bobbins

9 what thread is sold on

10 quilt and pillow in one

15 glass-head, flat, flower (e.g.)

18 seller of notions

19 embroidery and upholstery (e.g.)

21 gathering

22 quilter's candy store (2 wds)

24 material inventory

26 decorative element in a cake or quilt

27 a stitch that encloses the edge

DOWN

1 eighteenth-century sewing-tool keeper

2 repair a knit sock

3 to glue in fabric terms

4 a sample to test fit

5 what a zipper is called in England

6 held thirteen quilts in the olden days (2 wds)

11 high school sewing course (abbr, 2 wds)

12 used for threading elastic

13 snaps, hooks and eyes, hook-and-loop tape (e.g.)

14 knife edge (e.g.)

16 fusible or sew-in (e.g.)

17 female tailor

20 1930s sewist

23 bodkin box

25 sever a strand

26 fabric knee support

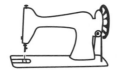

✦ Logic Puzzle 11

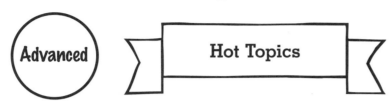

Advanced

Hot Topics

The Heritage Quilt Guild holds one theme meeting each month, at which a number of members gather to discuss different hot quilting topics. Using only the clues that follow, match each theme to the month in which it was discussed, the person who hosted the event, and how many total quilters were at each theme night.

1. The discussion in January was hosted by Teresa.

2. The meeting with 16 attendees was held sometime after the discussion hosted at Cindy's house.

3. The discussion hosted at Cindy's house was either "Modern versus Traditional Quilts" or "Sunbonnet Sue: Pros and Cons."

4. Of the discussion hosted at Joyce's house and "Sunbonnet Sue: Pros and Cons," one was held in March and the other had 12 attendees.

5. The topic in February was discussed by 13 quilters.

6. The meeting with 16 attendees was either the discussion hosted at Kristy's house or "Quilts in the Underground Railroad."

7. "Quilts in the Underground Railroad" was discussed either at the evening hosted at Teresa's house or the evening with 13 attendees.

		Themes				Hosts				Attendees			
		Modern versus Traditional Quilts	Domestic versus Longarm Machines	Quilts in the Underground Railroad	Sunbonnet Sue: Pros and Cons	Joyce	Kristy	Teresa	Cindy	10	12	13	16
Months	January												
	February												
	March												
	April												
Attendees	10												
	12												
	13												
	16												
Hosts	Joyce												
	Kristy												
	Teresa												
	Cindy												

Months	Themes	Hosts	Attendees
January			
February			
March			
April			

Solutions

✦ Logic Puzzle Sample—JUNE BUG QUILT MEETING

ORDER	QUILTER	PROJECT
1	Kerry	Anniversary quilt
2	Sue	Wallhanging
3	Betsy	Patchwork pillow
4	Alice	Baby quilt

♥ Crossword Puzzle 1—QUILT PARTS

Word Scramble 1—QUILT TYPES

AUTOGRAPH	STRING	RAG
SAMPLER	SCRAP	TRAPUNTO
ALBUM	MODERN	PICTORIAL
CHARM	MEMORY	ART
HAWAIIAN	CRAZY	SEMINOLE
MEDALLION	CHRISTMAS	
T-SHIRT	CIVIL WAR	

Word Scramble 2—FABULOUS FABRICS

BROADCLOTH	JACQUARD	CHIFFON	TULLE
DENIM	VINTAGE	MICROFIBER	GABERDINE
FLANNEL	MUSLIN	LINEN	GINGHAM
BATIK	VELVET	DAMASK	DOTTED SWISS
CHENILLE	TENCEL	WOOL FELT	EYELET
CORDUROY	FEED SACK	FRENCH TERRY	TICKING
HOMESPUN	POLYESTER	SILK	

♥ Crossword Puzzle 2
ACTION WORDS

♥ Crossword Puzzle 3—IT'S A MATTER OF TECHNIQUE

◣ Criss Cross 1—HAND QUILTING

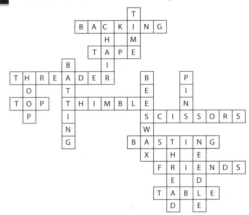

◣ Criss Cross 2—COLORS

✦ Logic Puzzle 1—WHITE GLOVE LADIES

VISITORS	VOLUNTEERS	EXHIBITS
25	Liz	Wearable art
50	Debbie	Wallhanging
75	Linda	Modern
100	Sue	Appliqué

✦ Logic Puzzle 2—INTERMEDIATE CLASSES

DATES	STUDENTS	QUILT CLASSES
July 12	Kristi	Free-motion quilting
July 15	Angela	Fabric dyeing
July 18	Roxane	Needle-turn appliqué
July 21	Dawn	Sewing curves

✦ Word RoundUp 1—QUILT QUESTIONS

```
Z B B B D K T H O I H O E L B U O D
L A M X V A I B G T H O Q X I Z R T
E T J Z D P T N F X J F U X E G W F
M R R L J C C P G E N G E J Q I P I
O I R L F H K S N H X C E A N E R O
Y N I A W X K Q D Y N G N I K C A B
N G F W G W C E Z W K L C R E K H
E Z P Y O I R I R U A Z N V U J S S
V A B R R E Z N S A W T O O T H F E
I A H X T J K D X Z H X P H N H A O
B T L I Q T J D E T T U B B U A G G
C H M T O P R Y P I H S D N E I R F
```

✦ Word RoundUp 2—QUILTING CONCERNS

```
V S V B Z W B B V S S R E H T O R B
O I Z S B L A N K E T S T I T C H N
X Z W H I T E P O S S Y D Q Z Q E C
F Y X F M A E C I R C L E A E S F
R Z M I K S I Y M B C Z N P D P U Y
N Z U T V W A E A Z T P F L Q S S X
M O R F S W H R U P U U R E R I K E W
Q A R S R C U W Q U E T E I T K S N V
M C E O R N Q Y B G U L L K H P O C
E R L A O E V U N R Z E I T K S N V
P O T R W Y V I N G E L U K D U A B
C S I B E E S W H B E R N I N A J W
```

◤ Quilt Block Word Mine 1—SHOOFLY

5-LETTER WORDS (3)
FOOLS
HOOFS
SHOOL

4-LETTER WORDS (8)
FOOL
HOLY
HOOF

HOYS
LOOS
OOHS
SHOO
SOLO

3-LETTER WORDS (10)
FLY
HOY
LOO

OHO
OHS
OOH
SHY
SLY
SOL
SOY

LO
OF
OH
OS
OY

2-LETTER WORDS (9)
HO

SH
SO
YO

◤ Quilt Block Word Mine 2—PINWHEEL

6-LETTER WORD (1)
NEPHEW

5-LETTER WORDS (6)
NEWEL
NEWIE
WHEEL
WHELP
WHILE
WHINE

4-LETTER WORDS (22)
ELHI

HEEL
HELP
HEWN
LIEN
LINE
LWEI
PEEL
PEEN
PEIN
PHEW
PILE
PINE
PLIÉ
WEEP
WHEE

WHEN
WHIN
WHIP
WILE
WINE
WIPE

3-LETTER WORDS (25)
EEL
EWE
HEN
HEP
HEW
HIE
HIN

HIP
LEE
LEI
LIE
LIN
LIP
NÉE
NEW
NIL
NIP
PEN
PEW
PHI
PIE
PIN

WEE
WEN
WIN

2-LETTER WORDS (8)
EH
EL
EN
HE
HI
IN
PI
WE

◤ Word Search 1—QUILT INSPIRATION

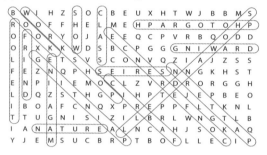

```
B W I H Z S O C B E U X H T W J B B M S
R O O F F H E L M E H P A R G O T O H P
O F O R Y O J A E Q C P V R B O O D D
R X K K W D S B C P G G N I W A R D
L G E T S V S C O N V Q Z I A J Z S S
F E Z N Q P H S E I R E S N N G K H S T
E N P I I E M O C L Z V R D R O R G G H
L D Q Z S T H G P H P T E J E P B E O
L B O A F C N Q X P R E P P F L T K N L
T U G N I S I Z I L B R L W N G T S L
I A N A T U R E A L N C A H J S O K A Q
Y J E M S U C B R P T B O F L L E C I P
```

❤ Crossword Puzzle 4—QUILT STYLES

(Crossword grid with answers including: POSTAGESTAMP, MARINERSCOMPASS, MINIATURE, INNOVATIVE, AMISH, LANDSCAPE, BALTIMOREALBUM, VINTAGE, STRING, STAINEDGLASS, TSHIRT, PAPERPIECED)

❤ Crossword Puzzle 5—QUILTERS KEEP BUSY

(Crossword grid with answers including: PROJECTLINUS, RESIDENCE, RETREAT, ASILOMAR, MINIGROUP, GUILD, SEWINGCIRCLE, GROUPQUILT, BLOCKSWAP, MAGAZINE)

♥ Crossword Puzzle 6—TOOLBOX

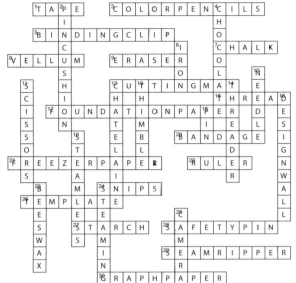

✳ Logic Puzzle 3—QUILTS OF DISTINCTION

YEARS	QUILTERS	QUILTS
1983	Harriet Hargrave	*Churn Dash Memories*
1991	Jane Hall	*Polka Dot Parade*
1999	Alex Anderson	*Stars in the Morning*
2007	Becky Goldsmith	*Symphony*
2015	Kathy Doughty	*Purple Treasure*

✳ Logic Puzzle 4—POSTAGE STAMP COMPETITION

PIECES	QUILTERS	GUILDS	PRIZES
4,320	Theresa	Lighthouse Quilters	First
5,184	Tristan	Full Moon Stitchers	Third
8,064	Lynn	Heritage Quilters	Viewer's choice
9,216	Zinnia	South Bay Sewists	Second

✎ Word Scramble 3—NOTIONS AND TOOLS GALORE

PINS
PINCUSHION
CHALK MARKER
SCISSORS
BEESWAX

NEEDLE
RULER
MAGNIFIER
TAPE MEASURE
SEAM RIPPER

THREADER
THIMBLE
STILETTO
GLOVES

PINKING SHEARS
SEWING GAUGE
WONDER CLIP

✎ Word Scramble 4—COLOR PLAY

ACID GREEN
BABY BLUE
AMBER
CELADON
BRICK RED
CHARTREUSE
BUBBLE GUM
FIRE-ENGINE RED
EGGPLANT
AMARANTH

CERISE
MINT
APRICOT
LEMON
BLUE
CADET BLUE
FUCHSIA
GOLDENROD
BARN RED
MIDNIGHT BLUE

ELECTRIC BLUE
LAVENDER
BLACK
SPRING GREEN
GUNMETAL
TOMATO RED
RUST
ORANGE
PERIWINKLE
TEAL

WINE
VIOLET
PEACH
OCHRE
EMERALD GREEN
PLUM
MAROON
ASH GRAY
APPLE

◤ Criss Cross 3—SEWING MACHINE FEET

◤ Criss Cross 4—MACHINE QUILTING

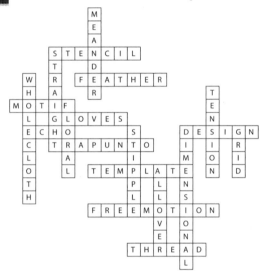

✖ Word RoundUp 3—FABRIC FANTASIES

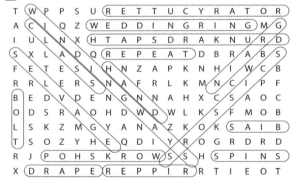

✖ Word RoundUp 4—SUPPLY SAFARI

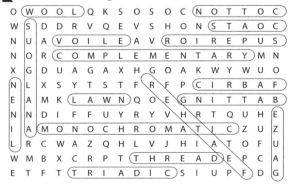

♥ Crossword Puzzle 7—FABRIC TYPE

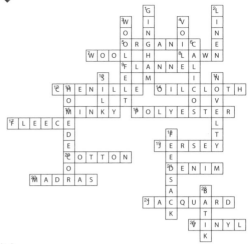

♥ Crossword Puzzle 8—BLOCKS 1

🧵 Quilt Block Word Mine 3—ALBUM

4-LETTER WORDS (5)	3-LETTER WORDS (7)	2-LETTER WORDS (6)
ALUM	ALB	AB
BALM	AMU	AM
BLAM	BAL	LA
LAMB	BAM	MA
MAUL	BUM	MU
	LAB	UM
	LAM	

🧵 Quilt Block Word Mine 4—JEWEL BOX

5-LETTER WORDS (5)			
BELOW	BOWL	JEE	WEB
BOWEL	JOWL	JOB	WEE
ELBOW	LOBE	JOE	WOE
JEBEL		LEE	
JEWEL	**3-LETTER WORDS (20)**	LEX	**2-LETTER WORDS (6)**
	BEE	LOB	EL
4-LETTER WORDS (6)	BEL	LOW	EX
BLEW	BOW	LOX	LO
BLOW	BOX	OLE	OW
BOLE	EEL	OWE	OX
	EWE	OWL	WE

🏴 Word Search 2—FIBER AND NEEDLE ARTS

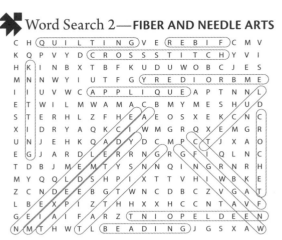

🏴 Word Search 3—TO DYE FOR

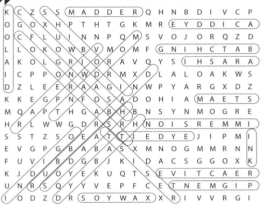

🌀 Word RoundUp 5—TEMPTING TERMINOLOGY

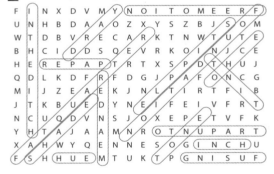

🌀 Word RoundUp 6—BEYOND BASICS

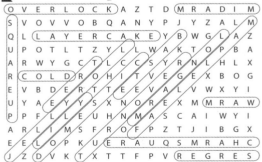

✦ Logic Puzzle 5—FABRIC SWAP

FAT QUARTERS	QUILTERS	COLORS
4	Jennifer	Green
6	Ruthmary	Yellow
8	Deirdre	Gray
9	Amy	White

76

✳ Logic Puzzle 6—SEWING FOR CHARITY

NUMBER OF ITEMS	QUILTERS	DONATIONS	TOWNS
2	Mai	Personal care kits	Montclair
4	Betsy	Baby quilts	Oakmore
6	Lucy	Walker caddies	Laurel
8	Alice	Pillowcases	Fruitvale

💜 Crossword Puzzle 9—BEST IN SHOW

💜 Crossword Puzzle 10—QUILTING TERMS

▸ Criss Cross 5—RETREATS

🌷 Quilt Block Word Mine 5—BASKET

5-LETTER WORDS (14)
ABETS
BAKES
BASTE
BATES
BEAKS
BEAST
BEATS
BETAS
SKATE
STAKE
STEAK
TABES
TAKES
TEAKS

4-LETTER WORDS (28)
ABET
BAKE
BASE
BASK
BAST
BATE
BATS
BEAK
BEAT
BEST
BETA
BETS
EAST
EATS
ETAS
KEAS
SABE
SAKE
SATE
SEAT
SETA
SKAT
STAB
TABS
TAKE
TASK
TEAK
TEAS

3-LETTER WORDS (18)
ABS
ASK
ATE
BAT
BET
EAT
KAB
KAS
KAT
KEA
SAB
SAT
SEA
SET
SKA
TAB
TEA
TSK

2-LETTER WORDS (5)
AB
AS
AT
BE
KA

📖 Word Scramble 5—GARMENT SEWING

PATTERN WEIGHTS
FRENCH CURVE
SHEARS
CHALK MARKER
TAPE MEASURE
PATTERN
SERGER

BUTTONS
ELASTIC
BIAS TAPE
SEWING GAUGE
ZIPPER
INTERFACING
HAM

IRONING BOARD
MARKING PENCIL
STRAIGHT PINS
PATTERN PAPER
INSTRUCTIONS

📖 Word Scramble 6—PATTERN PARADISE

NOVELTY
CHEVRON
HOUNDSTOOTH
GREEK KEY
PLAIN
GINGHAM
IKAT
CONVERSATIONAL
TARTAN

SOUTHWESTERN
SCROLL
QUATREFOIL
CAMOUFLAGE
FLEUR-DE-LIS
PAISLEY
ARGYLE
HERRINGBONE
SCALE

TOILE
PANEL
HARLEQUIN
GEOMETRIC
STRIPES
BORDER PRINT
POLKA DOT
BASKETWEAVE
BROCADE

▸ Criss Cross 6—DESIGN TOOLS

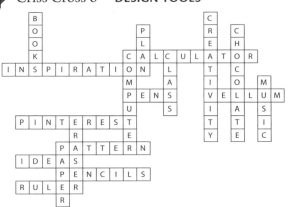

Criss Cross 7—QUILT COMPETITION

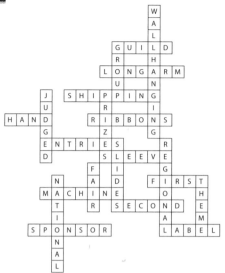

Crossword Puzzle 11—COLOR WHEEL

Crossword Puzzle 12—SEWING MACHINES

Logic Puzzle 7—QUILT RETREAT DELIVERIES

WEIGHT	QUILTERS	COLORS	BEDROOMS
35	Kerry	Red	Mountain Vista
38	Gailen	Black	The Victorian
41	April	Purple	The Cottage
44	Dina	Blue	The Fireplace Suite
47	Stacy	Plaid	The Ocean View

Logic Puzzle 8—QUILTER'S TRIVIA

SCORES	QUILTERS	DISHES	TOWNS
30	Miki	Prune whip	Walnut Creek
40	Meredith	Jello salad	Concord
50	Becky	Lasagna	Martinez
60	Dawn	Garlic bread	Pleasant Hill
70	Jen	Fruit platter	Lafayette

Word RoundUp 7—FABRIC FUN

Word RoundUp 8—SEWING STYLE

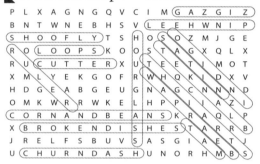

Word Search 4—ART QUILTING

Word Search 5—THINGS QUILTERS SEW

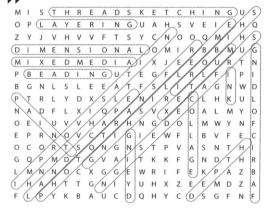

Crossword Puzzle 13—BLOCKS 2

Criss Cross 8—DESIGN IDEAS

Crossword Puzzle 14—FABRIC TERMS

Criss Cross 9—SEWING MACHINE PARTS

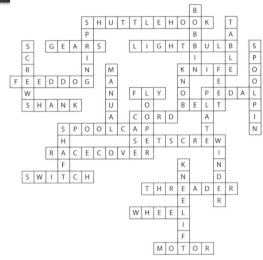

Logic Puzzle 9—QUILTING CONFERENCE

DAYS	QUILTERS	CLASSES
August 11	Sally	Quilt drafting
August 12	Tom	Curved piecing
August 13	Jackie	Improvisational piecing
August 14	Bill	Art quilting

Logic Puzzle 10—FIRST QUILTS

YEARS	NAMES	FIRST QUILTS
1983	Kennedy	Wallhanging
1984	Cynthia	Star block throw
1985	Jean	T-shirt quilt
1986	Kiki	Baby quilt
1987	Alice	Photo quilt

Word Scramble 7—TAN BY ANY OTHER NAME ...

FLESH
LIGHT APRICOT
VANILLA
BISQUE
EGGSHELL
LINEN
SNOW
SEASHELL
ECRU
SAND

WHEAT
ALMOND
BISCUIT
ALABASTER
CAMEL
BUFF
PEARL
WHITE CHOCOLATE
FAWN
CREAM

CORN SILK
LIGHT KHAKI
BEIGE
BONE
NAVAJO WHITE
CAFÉ AU LAIT
OATMEAL
CHAMPAGNE

Word Scramble 8—BLOCK PARTY

STARS AND STRIPES
BASKET
CHURN DASH
MISSOURI STAR
LEMOYNE STAR
SPIDERWEB
AIR CASTLE
JACOBS LADDER
IRISH CHAIN
SUNBONNET SUE

LOG CABIN
FOUR-PATCH
BEAR'S PAW
BLAZING STAR
PICKLE DISH
ORANGE PEEL
CROWN OF THORNS
KANSAS TROUBLES
CROSS AND CROWN
COURTHOUSE STEPS

ROSE OF SHARON
FLAGSTONES
WEATHERVANE
GOOSE TRACKS
HOUR GLASS
OHIO STAR
WHIG ROSE
RAIL FENCE
YANKEE PUZZLE
STORM AT SEA

Word RoundUp 9—PATTERN PLAY

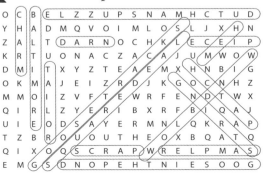

Word RoundUp 10 — BEAUTIFUL BASICS

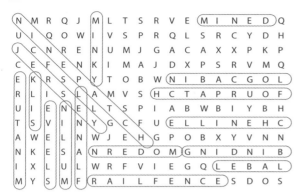

Quilt Block Word Mine 6 — HOUSE

4-LETTER WORDS (4)	3-LETTER WORDS (7)		
HOES	HOE	SUE	OH
HOSE	HUE	USE	OS
HUES	OHS	**2-LETTER WORDS (9)**	SH
SHOE	SHE		SO
	SOU	EH	UH
		HE	US
		HO	

Quilt Block Word Mine 7 — PINE TREE

7-LETTER WORDS (3)			
PRETEEN	PREEN	PIER	PEN
TEENIER	PRINT	PINE	PER
TERPENE	RENTE	PINT	PET
6-LETTER WORDS (8)	REPIN	PIRN	PIE
ENTIRE	RETIE	REIN	PIN
ENTRÉE	RIPEN	RENT	PIT
PTERIN	TEPEE	RETE	REI
REPENT	TERNE	RIPE	REP
REPINE	TREEN	RITE	RET
RETENE	TRINE	TEEN	RIN
TEENER	TRIPE	TERN	RIP
TRIENE	**4-LETTER WORDS (27)**	TIER	TEE
5-LETTER WORDS (18)	ÉPÉE	TINE	TEN
EERIE	ERNE	TIRE	TIE
ENTER	ITER	TREE	TIN
INEPT	NITE	TRIP	TIP
INERT	PEEN	**3-LETTER WORDS (22)**	**2-LETTER WORDS (6)**
INTER	PEER	ERE	EN
NITER	PEIN	IRE	IN
PETER	PENT	NÉE	IT
	PÈRE	NET	PI
	PERI	NIP	RE
	PERT	NIT	TI

Crossword Puzzle 15 — STITCHERY

Crossword Puzzle 16 — GENERAL SEWING

Logic Puzzle 11 — HOT TOPICS

MONTHS	THEMES	HOSTS	ATTENDEES
January	Quilts in the Underground Railroad	Teresa	10
February	Modern versus Traditional Quilts	Cindy	13
March	Sunbonnet Sue: Pros and Cons	Kristy	16
April	Domestic versus Longarm Machines	Joyce	12